SPECIAL PHOTOGRAPHY BY BILL BATTEN

FOREWORD BY JOSEPH ETTEDGUI

TEXT BY HELEN CHISLETT

IN TOUCH
TEXTURE IN DESIGN

KELLY HOPPEN

conran
OCTOPUS

Contents

FOREWORD BY JOSEPH ETTEDGUI

Our environment is an integral factor in the quality of life we lead. It affects our moods, our relationships and our wellbeing. We cannot always maintain the perfect environment, but we can surround ourselves with the colours, objects and fabrics that make us happy. Kelly Hoppen understands this completely; her work encompasses the spiritual and aesthetic dimensions of the world around us. She collects ideas from faraway places and filters them into the pure, understated style that has become her own. The textural qualities featured in this book focus on the qualities in our home that really matter: comfort, sensuality and stimulation.

To create, one has to be open to life. I need my home to be open to all that inspires me and helps me to create. Kelly Hoppen creates the essence of life in her interior design.

INTRODUCTION BY KELLY HOPPEN

I see this book as a journey – a textural odyssey that travels through many worlds. I would like to convince you that sensational interiors can be inspired by the ingredients of everyday life. Design to me is an organic process. Interiors magazines and glossy photographs can never excite the senses so much as opening your eyes to what is happening outside.

I always design with texture in mind: my signature style is to combine elements that you would not expect. Velvet becomes more luxurious when placed next to metal; clear glass appears more brilliant when placed next to opaque. There are no rules – you have total freedom.

Textures help you to recognise the hot and cold atmospheres within a home. Kitchens often feel harder and sharper in comparison to other rooms but it is possible to add natural ingredients that will warm them up, such as woods or woven baskets. Bedrooms should be sensual and warm: satins, velvets and suedes have a part to play in achieving this.

Feng shui recognises the importance to the senses of combinations of the elements: water, earth, metal, fire and wood. It highlights the importance of the materials you use and the way that energies can flow smoothly around the home. If you look at nature, you will see how this happens in an unforced way. Blossom against bark or reeds against a riverbank illustrate how textural contrasts occur naturally and yet dramatically. Accepting the power of such natural forces will take you a long way towards the creation of a happy home.

Interior design is not just a profession to me, but a passion. And where does my inspiration come from? From the earth itself.

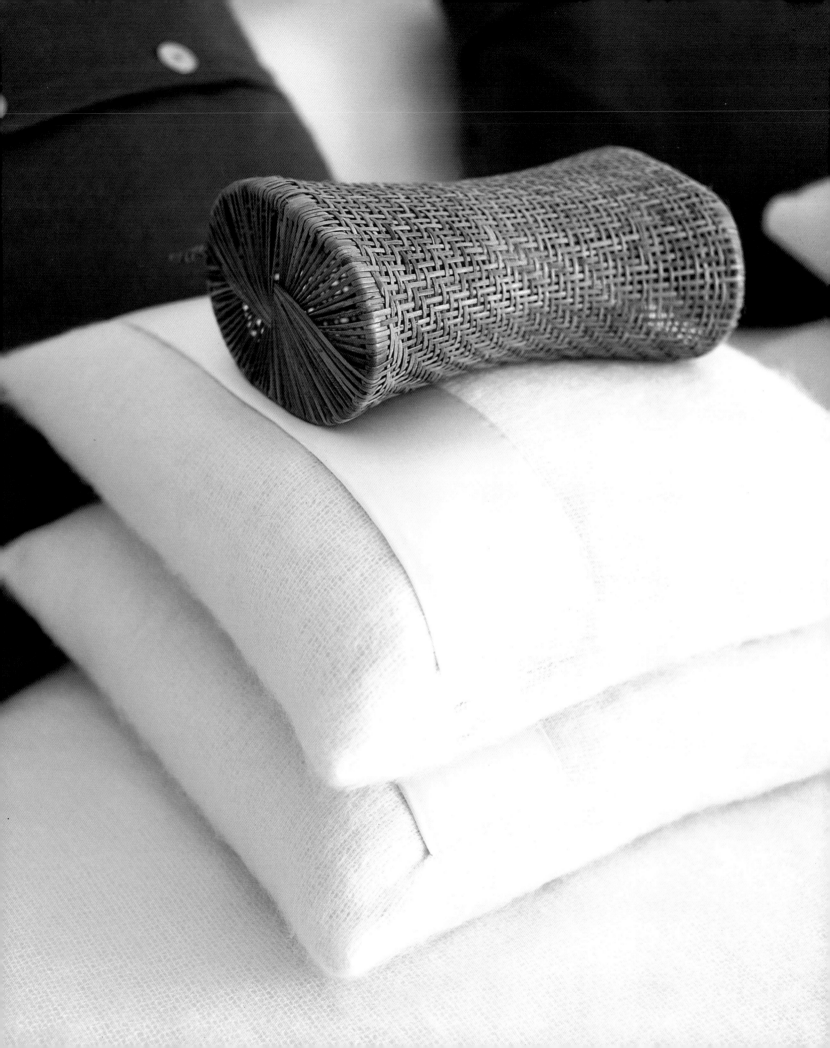

INSPIRATION

NATURAL & MAN-MADE

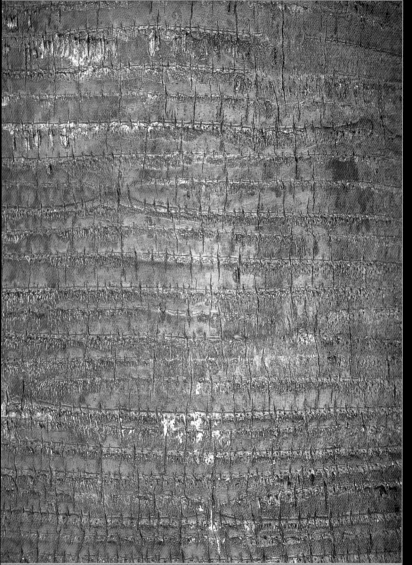

For me, inspiration is a subliminal thing. I gravitate towards geometric influences – parallel lines, squares and panels, for example, are recurrent themes in my work. While first appearing architectural, they are often an indirect response to nature – a field of wheat, stark winter trees, the ribbed vein of a leaf or the way light falls across a path. Images filter through all the time, stored consciously for later use.

To learn about textures, study nature to see how successfully they are mixed – lichen on stone, autumn leaves against bark, frost on grass, roses against a brick wall or rock pools filled with light. Wherever you turn there are combinations of hard and soft, light and dark, flimsy with firm, liquid with solid. These contrasts hold the secret to using texture effectively.

Let us take the big picture first: landscape. Catching the full glory of fields, hills, valleys, rivers, lakes or sea is both emotionally uplifting and artistically exciting. My eye is invariably drawn towards nature's patterns: the furrows of the field; the curves of the hill; the bend of the river. Then I start to take in the detail – the shape of a particular tree or the effect of water against earth. Rocks might resemble folds of fabric; streams become ribbons of satin.

The weather also plays its part in natural inspiration. Snow does magical things to the countryside by blanking out some things and focusing the eye on others. Look more closely and you will see unique forms and shapes appearing. Fog, rain, wind or brilliant sunshine all leave their own signature on the landscape and so open the mind to new possibilities.

NATURAL

When I am designing, images from nature come to mind, suggesting combinations of materials. I might search for a particular linen and then try it next to a satin. Rough and smooth both look and feel right; the combination reminds me of something I have experienced: a brilliantly clear winter's day with shining blue sky and skeletal trees; a brick path partly covered with snow, running alongside a rectangular pond that is frozen solid. The undyed linen I am holding is the snow, and the ice has become the smooth satin. Or I may choose to work with taffeta and wool – one stiff and crunchy, the other soft and dull. A memory of walking in a London park in autumn and suddenly becoming aware of the glorious colours and crunchiness of wet leaves underfoot has manifested itself in my choice of fabrics.

Light has a crucial part to play as well – it spotlights textural detail or casts dramatic shadows. Its impact on colour is well documented, but the same is true of its effect on texture. Without good lighting, any room will appear flat and uninteresting – no matter how well designed it might be. In my own schemes I have become fascinated with both the technicalities and the aesthetics of lighting. I like to incorporate concealed lighting purely to support fabrics and furnishings, making sure they are always seen at their best.

RIGHT

Nature teaches us to find beauty and contrasts of texture within the simplest forms – just study the way that stem, leaf and petals complement each other so perfectly. Seen silhouetted against the light, a flower takes on a wonderful serene, sculptural quality.

FAR RIGHT TOP

The ribbed veins of a leaf contrast with the translucent quality of the surface membrane.

FAR RIGHT MIDDLE

The landscape itself can be moulded into fascinating shapes by both man and nature.

FAR RIGHT BOTTOM

Unfurling petals show nature's fine attention to detail.

14

NATURAL

I also like to include lighting designs that are beautiful in their own right because of the patterns and shadows they cast on the walls and ceilings around them. Light effects in nature vary from the subtle to the spectacular, and directly influence the way I use light in my work. Imagine the soft, diffused light of a drizzly winter's day, or the great drama and spectacle of lightning cracking through a storm-darkened sky. I have seen a single shaft of brilliant white light breaking through clouds to spotlight a solitary tree, and a whole landscape brilliantly illuminated with gold as the sun wins the battle for supremacy after a storm.

Sometimes inspiration is direct – it was light that gave me the idea for putting metal runners on tables. I was working in my office one day when a beam of light came through the window and made a vertical line down the table. I immediately thought how beautiful it looked and realized I could copy the effect with a panel of metal on wood.

Opening your mind to the natural world is as much about paying attention to details as landscapes. The animal kingdom has always been a rich source of inspiration and materials. Fur, leather, feathers, shells and ivory are just a few examples of the range of materials that are favoured by designers today, many in synthetic versions. They have a strong visual appeal and are highly versatile in combination with other materials, but it is their tactile element that is their great strength and cannot be underrated. I watch people walk around rooms I have designed, and get a huge kick out of seeing them stroke things as they go. It is the response of their fingers as much as of their eyes that tells me I have succeeded.

LEFT
These smooth, black pebbles demand to be touched. They appear extra shiny when set upon a contrasting, grainier surface.
RIGHT
Rock formations are among the most fascinating of structures. Their colour, shape and texture can be integrated into the home by using stone floors in traditionally hard areas such as kitchens or bathrooms.

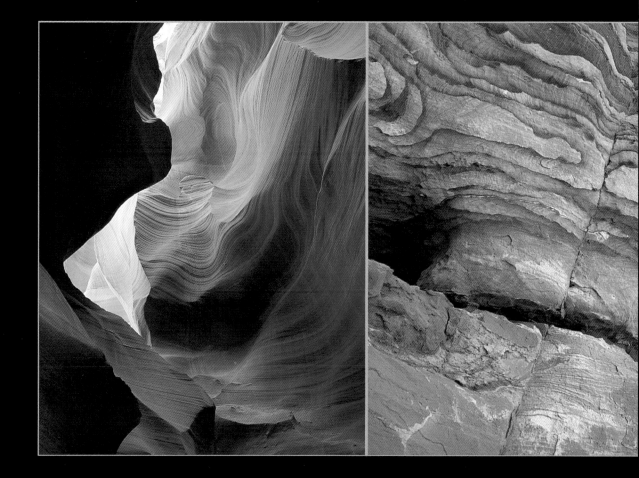

The animal and plant kingdoms also have more subtle gifts. The abstract beauty and infinite variety of shape, form, colour and texture offered by marine life, plants, animals, birds and insects is almost too broad to take in. The spiral pattern of a shell; the texture and colour of fish scales; the soft velvet of a rose petal; the sharpness of a thistle; the delicacy of a bee's wing and the irridescence of a butterfly. Focus on the roughness of bark, the smoothness of berries or the leathery quality of leaves. The scope for inspiration is endless.

Sometimes texture goes unnoticed because there is simply too much of it, and what should be clear becomes confused. Traditional Japanese gardens demonstrate what texture should be about, combining rocks, gravel, sculptural plants and water to create a calm and relaxing environment that is perfect for meditation. The mind settles on just one or two carefully controlled objects of natural beauty, rather than being dazzled by too much.

It is possible to learn the art of selectivity. Art gallery enthusiasts look at only a few paintings at any one time – if

19

Grasses, willows and twigs are among the most evocative forms in nature, because of the strong lines of light and dark they create against the landscape. Here they have a highly textural quality that is reminiscent of rough linen weaves, slatted shutters or latticed screens.

Bundles of willow form strong linear shapes that might inspire anything from a fabric to a furniture inlay. Build up layers of texture wherever possible – here a black horsehair ottoman has been teamed with a simple wooden bowl in which shiny porcupine quills are displayed.

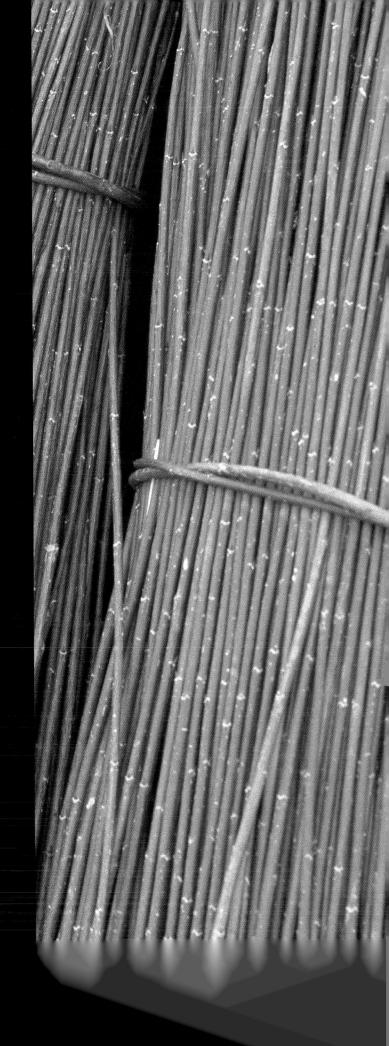

NATURAL

you rush around trying to see everything, you invariably remember nothing. The same is true when viewing nature. Concentrate on just one aspect of what you see; you will find that you notice and remember more.

Try to be aware, too, of how environments affect you. Most people feel serene and calm when surrounded by still water, while walking through woodland can heighten alertness. The art of feng shui recognizes the importance of combinations of water, earth, air, fire and wood in the home and the effect they have on the senses. It focuses on the materials used in order to allow energies to flow smoothly around the home. In nature, this happens in an unforced way. If you accept the power of such active and natural forces, it will take you a long way towards the creation of a happy and harmonious home.

MAN-MADE

It would be misleading to suggest that inspiration comes only from the natural world. Man's influence on his surroundings can be just as exciting. For me, urban life is a rich source of creative ideas – bricks, concrete, stone and glass have their own beauty, which should never be ignored.

The seasons can pass almost unnoticed when living in a town or city, so roads, pavements, walls, windows, traffic and artificial street lighting become the prominent features. But these should not be despised – open your mind to the effect of rain on asphalt when brightly lit; or the long shadows that railings cast; or the ingenuity of shop window designs. A walk down a street can give me an idea for a bedcover design or a mosaic pattern for a bathroom – not because I am looking consciously for inspiration, but because there are patterns all around if you see them and recognize them.

When you walk around a city, ideas can come from details in church gargoyles, complex brickwork, the shapes of chimneys. Even in rural settings, the hand of man is obvious – notice architectural styles, local materials, the way that buildings complement each other. All these things can help to feed your imagination.

The architecture in Paris always moves me. I find the buildings interesting to study – their constituent forms and shapes are fascinating – and I particularly appreciate the way the buildings are juxtaposed. As a city, it is impressively

ABOVE
A stunning black-and-white photograph by Hervé captures the mood of light and dark in the uncompromising Loggia at Marseille. The deep shadows cast on the concrete walls are an integral factor in the architect's unique vision.

RIGHT
Rooms can echo these architectural themes. The play of light with dark can be seen in this specially commissioned painting and on the table. The graphic qualities of black bring an edge to a room – here it frames the other components.

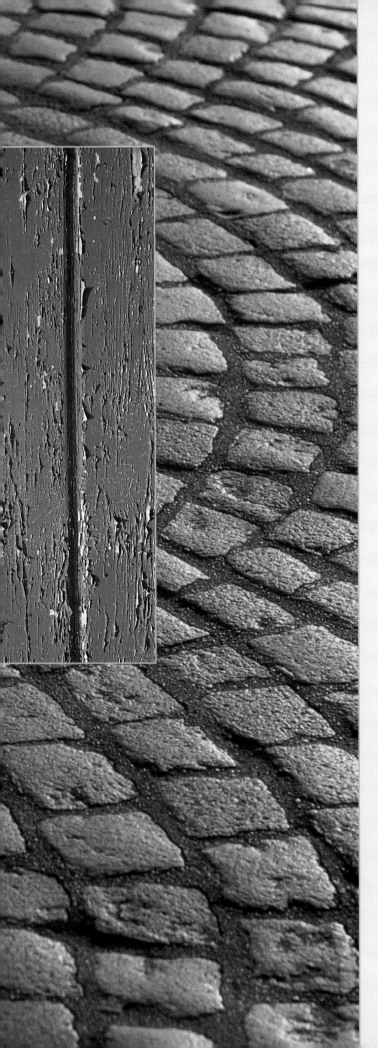

harmonious. There is also much to respect in the work of the great London architects – men such as Wren, Soane and Pugin – but I am just as likely to feel a huge rush of excitement when faced with a building of one of the great twentieth-century architects. I feel an affinity with much of the philosophy of modern architecture, playing down ornamentation and preferring to draw the eye towards the natural beauty of the materials. Adolf Loos, for example, was doing just this at the turn of the century. His Steiner House, built in 1910 in Vienna, is an absolutely pure building – quite shocking in its starkness.

The three materials that have revolutionized building construction this century are stainless steel, concrete and sheet glass. This combination produced the very first skyscrapers, and was responsible for the proliferation of high-rise architecture found in our cities today. Out of the three, sheet glass had the biggest effect on how the face of architecture changed. It resulted in lightness, transparency and structural daring, and a whole generation of architects was profoundly influenced by its possibilities. Among them was Mies van der Rohe, who set about designing buildings that would look like 'polished crystal'.

Le Corbusier had an equally uncompromising approach to his work. The Villa Savoye, built just outside Paris, was a pristine white box raised on twenty-six delicate columns, with

LEFT INSET

When displaying objects, think about how to build up textural interest. This stone console table is very rough and dull: the perfect foil for a pair of tortoiseshell boxes and an antique gilt mirror. The key box is by David Linley.

LEFT

Paving stones, distressed wooden surfaces and other architectural elements are a perennial inspiration. Look at the surfaces, the shapes and the patterns. Train yourself to observe textures everywhere.

long strips of sliding windows. The whole design played on transparency and opacity, closed form and open space.

This relationship between light and dark has been captured beautifully in the photography of Lucien Hervé, whose black-and-white prints of Modernist architecture expose this underlying tension. The roughness of concrete walls, the stark geometry of windows, the curve of stairwells and – most dramatically of all – the hardness of shadows, are as inspiring to me as ploughed fields or sea-drenched cobblestones. You do not have to love these buildings or want to live in them, but it is still worth trying to open your mind to the powerful statements they make.

Some of the best architecture in the world has been produced in the past two decades by Norman Foster and Richard Rogers. They and others in their generation profited from the technological expertise pioneered by their innovative predecessors. They recognized the aesthetic qualities of industrial materials, but then took design forward into an even more visually stimulating phase.

Of course it is not only architecture that continues to push back the frontiers when it comes to exploring new materials. Much architectural inspiration itself comes from a variety of areas – most noticeably industry. These inspirations have affected designers involved in furniture-making, interior design and other related fields. The trend has been to do away

FAR RIGHT INSET TOP
The ribbed, curved shape of this glass lampshade echoes that of glass-topped buildings.

FAR RIGHT INSET BOTTOM
These glass candlestick bases contrast with the plain wood on which they stand.

RIGHT
Strengthened glass has revolutionized architecture over the last 150 years. From the glass domes of the nineteenth century to today's skyscrapers, it dominates more prosaic materials. Light is now a major factor in design.

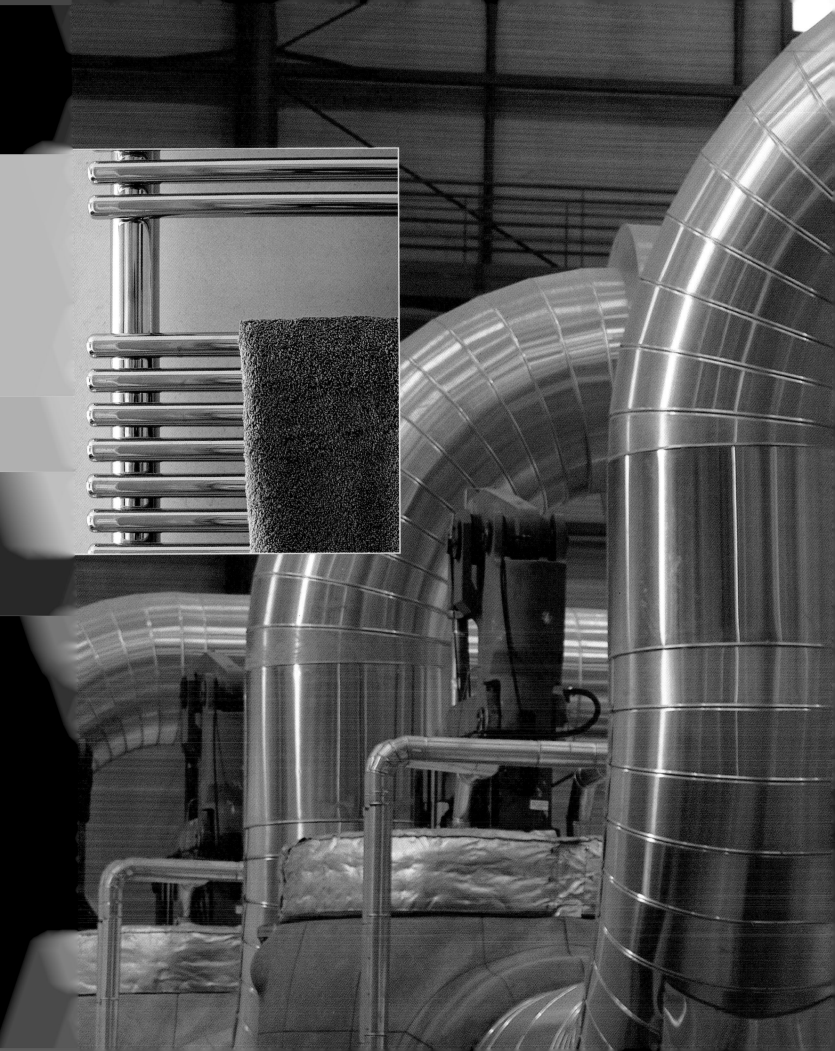

with ornamentation and focus instead on form and function. So industrial-style materials – concrete, steel, aluminium, glass and exposed brick – have found a new relevance in our homes. Initially this resulted in loft-style apartments that looked more like factories than houses, but today those elements have been refined and given a sophisticated edge. Clients are often surprised when they realize how wide the range of components I have used in a room can be, and that some elements are traditionally found on construction sites.

What is so exciting from a design point of view is how all these influences have filtered through to related disciplines. In furniture design, makers are combining metals, leathers, woods and fabrics to give an exciting new edge to the craft. The same goes for textiles, where improved technology means that anything goes: feathers, ribbons or rubber, for example. Suedes, velvets, silks, linens and satins have been reinterpreted – crushed, twisted, shredded or braided – so as to be in keeping with the new approach. In flooring, rubber, aluminium and leather are now on the market. Improvements in synthetics mean that convincing artificial copies are available for most things – and at half the original price.

These are exciting times for anyone who loves design. Technological discoveries made over a hundred years ago are still making waves today. And as we enter a new millennium, it really is time to look to the future.

LEFT INSET	LEFT
Industrial design has become an accepted part of domestic life over the past thirty years. This stainless steel radiator and towel holder combines function with aesthetics, its bold horizontals making a strong visual impact.	*Gargantuan stainless steel pipes twist and bend around a factory floor. Designers have taken inspiration from scenes such as this to find ways of introducing strong, uncompromising materials into the home environment.*

FASHION

BELOW LEFT AND RIGHT
The cut and style of a garment can inspire anything from the shape of a curtain to more ornamental detailing. Take a close look at the masterly cut of couture tailoring for inspiration. Here, the curves and folds of heavy silk curtains tied with braid echo the gathered fabric of an Issey Miyake dress.

It used to be the case that fashion came first and then, a few years later, interiors followed suit. Now the boundaries have become blurred – fashion designers often use materials traditionally associated with furnishings and many have even launched their own interiors brands; while design for the home is influenced by the clothes seen on the catwalk. In one of his collections, John Galliano used *ikat* – a tapestry-style fabric more usually associated with mediterranean beach houses. Needless to say, it looked fabulous in his clothes. Issey Miyake's famous pleats have been copied by every major fabric company and are available for a variety of home furnishings, and the elegant, tailored style of an Armani suit is commonplace in our living rooms.

It comes as no surprise then to see how much of a role texture plays in both worlds. Fashion offers everything from the diaphanous designs of Voyage and Galliano to the luxury

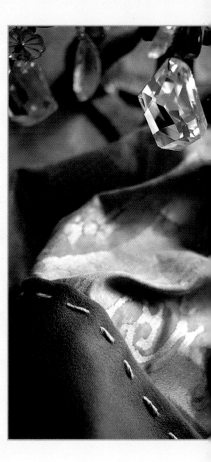

LEFT
A sumptuous evening dress, such as this Hervé Leger design, can be the catalyst for a number of decorative interior design ideas.
BELOW
This felt and Fortuny cloth has been carefully stitched with gold thread – a touch that emphasizes the magnificence of one fabric and the elegant simplicity of the other.

of Pashmina scarves and ostrich-skin bags. We have seen Ralph Lauren teaming combat trousers with silk ponchos, and Antonio Berardi's wayward collections of chiffon skirts, embroidered suits and mohair dresses. Nicole Farhi has offered linen skirts with leather coats, while at Chloé Stella McCartney has mixed satin skirts, chiffon dresses and embroidered boleros. Read any fashion editor's columns right now and you will find that these combinations of texture – as opposed to skirt length or colour – are the big stories.

Fashion's shock tactics have played a part in pioneering new technologies and materials that have created opportunities across the design world. They have also opened our minds to the fact that a table does not have to be made of wood, just as a dress does not have to be made of cotton.

Inspiration for me might come from the slubby weave of men's suit fabric, the precise detail of couture tailoring, a pink brocade coat by Galliano – these could be transformed respectively into cushion trims, a dining chair cover or an attention-seizing pair of curtains. However, the creative process is usually less direct and I benefit from a general awareness of what is happening in the world of fashion.

Not that texture is a new thing in fashion or homes. Velvets, furs, leathers and embroidery were all a feature of medieval dress. Brocades and silks were introduced when explorers returned from the Far East. Fortuny dresses were a sensation in their day, and are still much copied. But it is the later years of the twentieth century that have been the most inventive where materials for clothing are concerned.

LEFT AND RIGHT
Not all the connections made between fashion and decoration are obvious. Think about the mood that certain clothes create – then take that as the starting point for the ambience of a room. The strong lines of this black-and-white Hervé Leger bodice, for example, are echoed in these ironwork banisters against the cream carpet. The black borders emphasize the dramatic curve of the stairway and the shape of each step.

FASHION

In the 1930s, designer Elsa Schiaparelli was among the first to begin experimenting with materials such as Cellophane, glass and parachute silk. Her different textural adventures inspired designers in the 1960s, such as Paco Rabanne, who created space age clothes with metals and plastic. More recently, Issey Miyake's striking sculptural clothes seem to have echoes of Fortuny within them. Designers are now experimenting with stainless steel, rubber bands, newspaper, wood, glass and even thistledown, to push the frontiers of fashion to the limit.

There are strong emotional undertones in these choices of material, so it comes as no surprise to see how the art world has invaded fashion in search of new media with which to convey subtle messages. Young artists are using materials such as gauze, voile, net and feathers to evoke the ephemeral and transient mood of the late 1990s, while the rattan body that Miyake produced in the 1980s suited the hardness and inflexibility of that decade.

With such a fertile cross-pollination of ideas between fashion, art and interior design, this is an exciting time. Fashion designers love to use the rough with the smooth, the matt with the shiny, metallics with naturals, just as I do when creating a room. The pages of *Vogue* could hold just as much inspiration for your home as any interiors magazine.

RIGHT

Fashion has always led the way in textile design – sexy, shimmering cloths such as this one used by Issey Miyake have long been part of the fashion designer's palette. New technology means that the same textile effects can be created for the modern home.

FAR RIGHT AND INSET

Metallic surfaces have moved out of the fashion world and into interior design – this silver foil wallpaper creates a stiking semi-reflective surface that has the sensuality of a silver sheath dress. The dark wood of the vase adds a natural element.

34

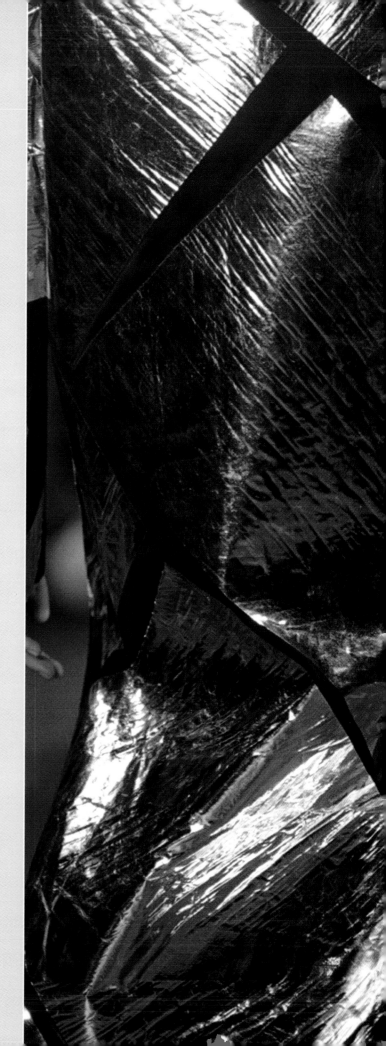

INGREDIENTS

SMOOTH & ROUGH

OPAQUE & SHEER

MATT & GLOSSY

HARD & SOFT

MATERIALS DIRECTORY

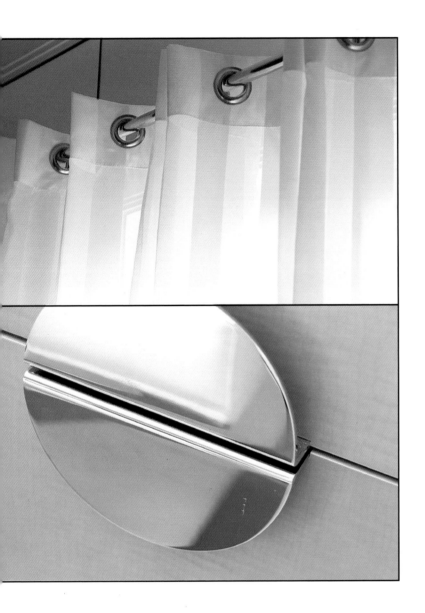

INTRODUCTION

It is not enough to find inspiration – the next step is to translate it into your own decorative scheme. Consider the images you have collected and the direction you would like to take – then analyse what that means in textural terms.

At its simplest, this is a question of contrasting hard with soft, rough with smooth, and so on. Now you have to find the decorative equivalent of those items – perhaps light and shadow become steel and wood; or water on rock becomes satin against tweed. Take these ingredients and layer them up within a room so that you have a wealth of textural contrasts. It is a totally new way of thinking, but you will soon realize how creatively liberating using texture can be.

Remember that contrast is the key word here. A shimmering sheer will look more fragile when juxtaposed with slubby linen; the glitter of glass will be diamond hard against the deep matt intensity of wenge, a dark, heavy wood from the African continent. Sometimes you need only an accent to gain maximum effect – gold stitching on felt, for example.

You can also use texture to alter the atmosphere of certain rooms. Natural ingredients such as wood or woven baskets will help to soften the traditional hard lines of a kitchen and create warmth. Similarly, luxurious satins, velvets and suedes will help to make a bedroom feel sensual and inviting. We can use texture to create personal sanctuaries in an increasingly hostile world. Our havens are enriched when we borrow from outside to influence our choice of materials.

ABOVE TOP AND BOTTOM

Assess the role of each ingredient in your scheme – be it the transparency of voile curtains or the mirrored surface of a nickel handle – and where best to place it. Clever juxtaposition is the key to success.

RIGHT

A view of the whole room shows how the ingredients work together to build up a serene atmosphere. The voile does not just affect the windows, but casts shadows on the floor, adding another layer of interest.

SMOOTH & ROUGH

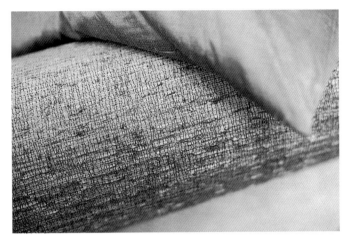

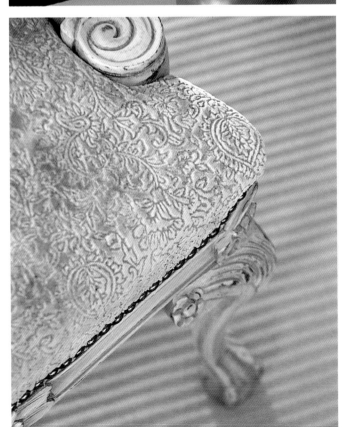

LEFT TOP
Fabrics offer so many textural contrasts that they are a good place to start when designing a room. This rough chenille has been teamed with raw silk for a tactile effect.

LEFT MIDDLE
The ornate gilded frame of this antique mirror has a sculptural quality. The polished surface of a silver cup contrasts with it perfectly, and is reflected in the mirror for double impact.

LEFT BOTTOM
A specially commissioned velvet perfectly complements the colour and texture of this carved chair.

One sense that has been brought to the forefront in our homes today is touch. Who can explain why it gives us such satisfaction to feel the roughness of one object and then the smoothness of another? I suspect it all goes back to what we experienced as babies: the clothes and fabrics we were surrounded by. Just think of traditional baby blankets – knitted wool with edges of satin. Perhaps there is a subliminal recognition in interior design today that we need to feel safe in our homes, cocooned from harm. The textures that once made us feel secure can do so again.

Of course, the eye takes as much satisfaction from such combinations as our tactile sense. A window is the perfect place to experiment with this notion. I might team coarse linen blinds with cascading satin curtains, or pick up on the idea of those baby blankets and edge pure cotton sheets with satin ribbon. Tweed and silk banners could frame a doorway. Soft furnishings should be rich in texture – chenille trimmed with leather, or velvet with carpet binding.

You might find that you have already unconsciously teamed smooth with rough. It could be a coarse upholstery fabric

ABOVE

The strong lines of this chenille-and-silk fabric give this armchair a strong, graphic quality. They also emphasize the rough and smooth elements inherent in the cloth.

41

against the polished wood of a chair, a pile of wonderfully thick towels on a marble surface or a collection of smooth polished pebbles in a stone dish. The contrast exaggerates the texture: smooth things appear smoother and rough things rougher. And if the chair appears more deeply polished, the marble shinier, and the pebbles more beautiful, they will be irresistible to touch.

In rooms that are texturally all the same, the effect is very bland – just as it would be if everything were the same colour. There is no sense of a room being built up through layers, which gives it interest and depth. Learn to focus on surface texture rather than colour.

Take a look around your home and experiment a little by moving objects and furniture around, not with colour in mind but with texture. Think about the concepts of smooth and rough, and see whether there are any small changes you could make that will bring these to the fore. Perhaps you could lay a runner over a table, or edge curtains or bedlinen with a contrasting fabric. Think about making a centrepiece with objects of shining beauty – marbles, polished stones, pieces of glass, Indian door knobs. Then frame them by placing them on the coarsest surface you can find. By starting with small alterations, you can learn how to create the most satisfying effects and you will build up the confidence to make big decorating decisions.

LEFT
Maximum visual impact is achieved here by placing antique tortoiseshell boxes on the roughened surface of a stone console table. To bring attention to a distressed surface, highlight it with shiny, smooth objects.

RIGHT TOP
Wood veneers can be chosen for textural contrast – as with this David Linley cabinet.
RIGHT MIDDLE
Leather can be used as sensuous upholstery.
RIGHT BOTTOM
This chic beechwood table has been inlaid with leather.

OPAQUE & SHEER

The density or transparency of a material determines how much light it lets through. It is for this reason that the juxtaposition of opaque and sheer is so interesting in interiors. Until a few years ago, only a handful of architects and designers took these concepts into the domestic setting. Most houses were – and still are – built only with standard plate glass. But today it is possible to order all kinds of glass and different laminated surfaces for use both externally and internally. When opaque glass is used, less light is allowed in and it is more difficult to see through. With the increased privacy this offers, curtains or blinds are optional – so they can be used purely with visual impact, rather than function, in mind.

Internally, opaque surfaces are the perfect companion to lighting effects. Walls, screens, internal windows and doors can all be made from opaque materials – the bright light on one side will be softly diffused on the other. Lighting designers emphasize this trend with decorative shadow effects that can bring a subtle new dimension to a room. Bedrooms and bathrooms are the natural places to experiment with this idea, as these rooms should be the most sensuous. Remember, too, that the sparkling transparency of clear glass is more brilliant when it is placed next to its frosted equivalent.

RIGHT
Sandblasted glass is a contemporary and effective way of using combinations of transparency and opacity in a room. Here the rectangular panels have been designed to echo the geometric shapes elsewhere in the room. The clear glass emphasizes the effect.

FAR RIGHT ABOVE
Semi-transparent curtains are the perfect partner for this pair of cashmere cushions, which look dark and solid against the light.

FAR RIGHT BELOW
A pale wooden objet d'art by William Yeoward is positioned in front of gauzy curtains to accentuate the textures of both.

44

OPAQUE & SHEER

FAR LEFT

A moveable screen, such as this panelled wenge and rattan version, is a versatile way of introducing opacity and solidity into a room. Not only is it a flexible piece of furniture that can be used to break a room up into zones, but it can also be positioned to benefit from the changing natural light within a room. Traditional Japanese interiors often used large paper screens to divide rooms according to how they were being used. The diffused light creates a sense of calm.

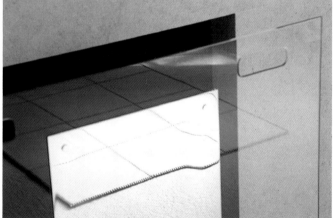

LEFT ABOVE

Technological advances now allow sandblasted glass to be made into shutters. This is a simple way of substituting opaque glass for clear – the window panels behind bring a geometric element into the room.

LEFT BELOW

Glass is being used in increasingly unexpected ways, as shown by this glass firescreen with nickel mesh inlay. Glass furniture is also becoming increasingly popular again, often designed to incorporate metal or stone.

Just as windows always had clear glass, so sheer fabrics were once synonymous with net curtains. But happily even these have shaken off their suburban image in recent years. Fabric manufacturers now offer fabulous ranges of sheers, some so glamorous they could be used for lingerie. No longer confined to white synthetic, they have now blossomed into all manner of silks, chiffons, gauzes, organzas and lace. Many are snipped and shredded so that the light comes through them and casts intricate shadows on the floor. Their role is to bring something flimsy and ephemeral into a room. By placing them next to solid textiles such as velvet, suede or linen, you emphasize the contrasting qualities of each. Just as putting rough objects with smooth ones accentuates the

contrast, you can position transparent with solid. Do not restrict this idea to fabrics: the transparent element could be a pierced wooden screen or blinds made of feathers.

You could start by looking at the cushions you have at home. Materials once only found in fashion houses are now widely available and can easily be made into simple cushion covers. Combining different weaves and layers of sheer fabrics will produce a variety of effects. Think about creating a new look for windows by framing them with soft tresses of sheer fabric. Alternatively, experiment with opacity by buying a Japanese-style screen and placing a lamp behind it. From there, it will be a short step to reconsidering existing surfaces and questioning how their full potential can be achieved.

MATT & GLOSSY

LEFT TOP
The glint of a gold fan emphasizes the gloss of this curved glass.

LEFT MIDDLE
The smooth surface of this bowl is set off by the dullness of the matt radiator cover.

LEFT BOTTOM
Opaque glass handles on plain glass doors are a simple contrast.

ABOVE
The lustre on these beautiful gold-rimmed antique glasses has been highlighted by positioning them against matt walls on a very contemporary plain glass shelf. This creates a modern still life, playing up the contrast of old and new as well as textures.

The terms matt and gloss were once used to describe only one thing: paint. Matt was for walls and gloss for woodwork. But recent years have seen a shift away from this idea – eggshell, as opposed to gloss, has become the sophisticated choice for many home owners who prefer the more intense nature of matt colours. Paint manufacturers now offer all kinds of products for decorating surfaces, some of which place the emphasis on something other than colour. Glossy metallic glazes to use over matt walls are just one example of how the boundaries have become blurred. These are particularly interesting because they offer decorators the opportunity to introduce another element to paint colour, by imposing shininess on matt through a stripe, square or circle of glossy glaze. It is a form of applied decoration that looks set to overtake the fashion for more obvious techniques, such as colourwashing or stencilling.

The subtlety of this idea is in keeping with the way decoration is moving forward. There is a recognition that – like smooth and rough, matt and glossy – they bring another layer of interest. Wall surfaces are only one example. Not long ago the only decision was what colour to paint them. Now we are more likely to consider the texture: the polished-plaster look of an Italian palazzo perhaps, or something subtle, resembling soft talc. The same is true of floors – polished wood floors can be teamed with deep-pile velvety rugs. In this way, wood becomes even shinier and velvet more luxurious.

The contrast between matt and glossy can be taken into every area within the home. You might use opaque glass against clear; metal against wood (like my signature steel runners on tables); distressed leather against clear plastic; slub silk against horn. It might mean flannel cushion covers with mother-of-pearl buttons, or tweed upholstery on metal chairs. At its simplest, it is a brilliantly clear glass vase filled with flowers. At its most complex, it is an entire scheme designed around these two textural ingredients.

A good starting point is to consider the paint finishes you have used. Consider whether your choice of matt or gloss was determined by conscious thought or habit. What difference might it have made had you chosen other finishes? Is the eye drawn by colour or by the intrinsic beauty found in the surface itself? Are the walls simply flat or do they offer some sort of textural interest?

Now open your mind to what else is going on in the room. Look at the windows and how they are dressed, then move on to consider the floor, the furniture, the accessories. Think hard about the surfaces of all of these things and the juxtapositions within the room. Once you have surveyed the existing scheme, you might find you have some ideas on how to improve it – perhaps with the introduction of paint glazes, floor varnish, or one new piece of glossy, glamorous furniture that will act as a focal point in the room.

LEFT ABOVE AND BELOW
A wenge table creates a dark canvas on which to display more glittering objects. Here, the dark inlay makes a backdrop for miniature candles and bales of moss. Glasses of leaves and stems create a tableau of shape and texture.

RIGHT
Today's design philosophy means taking a lateral view when thinking about additional touches. In this large glass vase, lilies have been submerged in water – a contemporary twist that brings out their inherent fragility.

HARD & SOFT

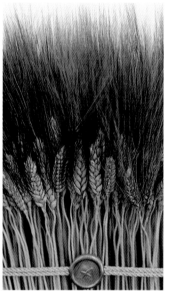

Design is all to do with making hundreds of individual choices and selections, and still being able to hold in mind what their overall impact will be. Shapes and lines fascinate me and are very much a signature within my work, so when I am putting a scheme together, I am concerned not just with colour and pattern, but with the graphic nature of the finished result. How things feel plays a vital role in my work, and hard and soft play an important part in this. But they are more significant in terms of the lines that are created within a scheme – the hard edges of solid furniture or the unstructured softness of swathes of fabric.

It is always important to get the hard bones of a room right: the floorboards, picture rails, cornicing, doors, windows and valances. This forms the canvas on which you work – the setting for everything else. Furniture shapes also set the tone – the chunkiness of a table, the squareness of a sofa, the height of a headboard or the depth of shelving. I see these as linear elements, and their positioning is absolutely vital. I like to bring a sense of geometry to a room, which is why I often favour symmetry – a pair of lamps at each side of a sofa perhaps, or groups of pictures that form rectangles on walls. These are confident statements which set the tone of the

FAR LEFT TOP
Grains or grasses bring a natural, organic softness into the home.

LEFT TOP
Cut like a diamond to reflect light, this banister finial is hard and sharp next to the dullness of the wood.

LEFT BOTTOM
The soft folds of these generous curtains contrast with the bold shadows on the floor.

RIGHT
Fabrics are pivotal in a scheme – not just because they are soft and tactile, but also because they blur sharp edges. This dark table looks even more solid when teamed with a luxurious fabric. Echoing this theme are the thick folds of curtain fabric against the plain wooden floor.

ABOVE

*The elegant shape of
this metal lamp creates
a dramatic effect
against a silk screen.
Lighting plays a very
important role. Choose
lamps both for their
specific lighting effects
as well as their own
inherent design.*

design – the equivalent of an artist's line drawings or a gardener's flowerbeds.

However, the hard edges need to be knocked off a little when designing warm, relaxed and comfortable homes. This is where the soft elements come in – fabrics, rugs, cushions, lampshades, plants. These might still echo the shapes first introduced – certainly rugs and cushions do – but they do not have such definition of line, being made of softer materials. As with the other ingredients mentioned so far, their success lies in the contrast – hard lines become more definite when seen against a backdrop of billowing fabric; airy fabric

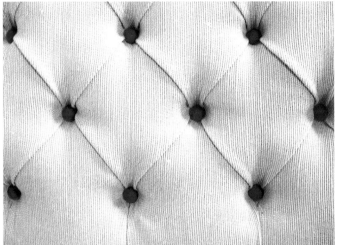

appears more floaty when juxtaposed with sharp edges. Think of wrought iron teamed with Fortuny fabric, or steel partnered with rich slubby silk.

This excites the eye and encourages our tactile sense. Fingers are drawn towards such an interesting environment – particularly the sensual softness of fabrics. Mohair and cashmere are among my favourites because they live up to expectation when you stroke them – as do fur, suede or velvet. You needn't spend a fortune – but budgeting to include a couple of luxurious cushion covers or some throws can make all the difference.

When assessing your own home, look to see what shapes or lines are already in place. Is there a way of repositioning furniture to accentuate these? Perhaps by investing in a couple of bold lamps, side tables or bay trees you could make a symmetrical feature. Then you can look for ways of contrasting the hard with the soft through a glorious choice of fabrics and accessories.

LEFT TOP

This driftwood console table by John Makepeace is rich and grainy. Draw attention to the roughness of a surface like this with something clear and polished, such as a glass dish.

LEFT SECOND DOWN

Attention to detail makes the difference between an acceptable and a superlative decorative scheme. Here rich velvet buttons on a linen cloth add the all-important finishing touch.

LEFT THIRD DOWN

Suede is such a sensuous material that it has taken on a new relevance in today's interiors – here a cupboard door has been covered in deep blue suede, which is complemented by gold upholstery nails.

LEFT BOTTOM

This line of studs creates a border around a simply covered chair – the shiny hardness of the nail heads is a pleasing contrast to the plump fabric.

MATERIALS DIRECTORY

In the previous chapter I discussed the general principles of using texture. Here I have compiled my list of textural essentials for decorators. This includes not only the materials themselves, but also brief descriptions of how to use them to best effect in your home.

Some of the materials are inexpensive and widely available, but there is no need to be disheartened if you feel that others – such as cashmere, silk and marble – are well beyond your budget. In fact, inexpensive versions of nearly everything listed here are available – it is just a question of using your imagination and shopping around. Architectural salvage yards and street markets are excellent sources of interesting materials, which are often unique and inexpensive. What is more important is to take the lessons learnt in the first two chapters, and look at how to introduce the textural equivalent

of some of these items into your own schemes. Also remember that you can make a little of something go a long way if you are clever. Trimmings, buttons and other decorative fripperies are excellent ways of bringing in a taste of glamour and luxury, and these often highlight textural contrasts, too.

If money is no barrier, then allow yourself to be totally indulgent – particularly in rooms which are very special, such as the bedroom and the bathroom. Once you have trained your mind to move away from decisions based on colour and pattern, and instead started to follow the textural path, you will never look back. Some of these combinations are so seductive that, once discovered, you simply can't let them go again. Take the time to explore all of the possiblities. I can guarantee the result will be a home that is as wonderfully sensuous as it is beautiful.

ALCANTARA

This is an excellent alternative to suede which simulates the look and the feel but is far more cost-effective. It also comes in a similar choice of colours and finishes to real suede. Alcantara can be used for all kinds of furnishings, including cushions, throws and trims. Try combining it with contrasting fabrics, such as satin, to emphasize the qualities in both.

CALICO (MUSLIN)

This is an inexpensive material that is also highly versatile – calico can be used anywhere and for just about anything. It is an excellent neutral for banners, runners and blinds. Try teaming it with an unexpected luxury – cashmere, perhaps, or silk – to give it a more contemporary twist.

CARPET

With the recent trend for wooden floors, carpets have suffered something of a decline in popularity. However, they are beginning to make a comeback as comfort once again becomes a priority in the home. Use them for living room and bedroom floors or any room where you want guests to

feel comfortable enough to sit on the floor, should they wish. Wool and wool-blend carpets are preferable to artificial fibres as they provide greater comfort and durability. Other materials, such as sisal and seagrass, have greater textural appeal and are excellent floor coverings.

CASHMERE

This is the softest and one of the most luxurious of fabrics available. Use cashmere where it will be close to you and you can enjoy the feel of it – cushions, blankets and throws, even hot water bottle covers. Try accentuating its softness by partnering it with something coarse, such as tweed. Cashmere is expensive, but you can make a

little go a long way by combining it with less expensive materials such as calico (muslin).

COTTON

The simplicity and versatility of cotton – an endless variety of colours, patterns and textures – makes it the perfect foil for a luxurious material such as taffeta. It has lost its rustic image in recent years and is still excellent value. Make the most of different weights and textures, from denim to muslin, and use it imaginatively.

CREWEL WORK

This embroidered fabric comes mainly from India, and was once found in only the most traditional of homes. However, in recent years its weight and the intricacy of its designs have made it popular. Neutral, self-coloured examples are particularly useful, as the decoration relies purely on texture. Use it in small spaces to really make an impact.

FELT

This is a good alternative to wool as it shares many of the same opaque qualities, but at a fraction of the price. It also comes in a fantastic array of shades. The secret of using felt and still retaining a sense of luxury is to lift it with more expensive trimmings.

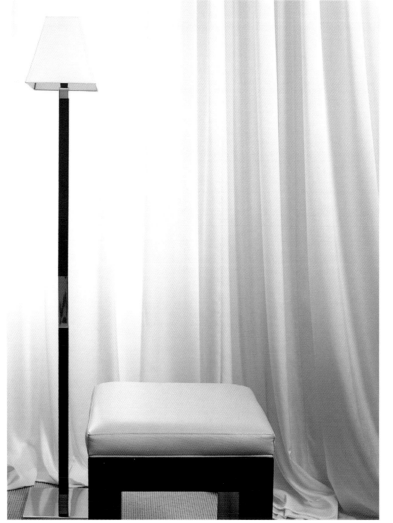

GLASS

Technological advances in the glass industry have opened up new possibilities for using glass in the home. Use sandblasted or clear glass to emphasize an opaque finish. Designs can be custom-made for your home. It is also suitable for interior screens as well as windows and doors.

GRANITE

Organic is one of the key words in interiors, and there are few materials more beautiful than rock. It has the advantage of being practical as well as aesthetically pleasing and it is ideal in kitchens, dining rooms and bathrooms. Granite is at its most effective when teamed with materials such as wenge or stainless steel.

HAND-COLOURED OR CUSTOM-MADE FABRICS

Soft furnishings have made great advances in recent years and it is now possible to have designs custom-made to your own specifications and colour choices. It is an expensive service, but it can make all the difference if you are determined to achieve a certain effect.

HORN

Another natural material with a great deal of textural interest. It does not need to be used in large quantities – horn buttons on cashmere cushions, for example, are the perfect finishing touch to a luxuriously indulgent scheme. Beakers, cutlery and candle holders made of horn are another subtle way of introducing it into a scheme.

INNOVATIVE FABRICS

There is now a whole host of fabrics manufactured specifically for texture rather than for colour – shredded, pleated, twisted, embossed, to name just a few of the varieties available. These fabrics can be used in the home wherever their originality will be best emphasized.

LEATHER

Once found only on armchairs in offices and studies, leather has now muscled into other key areas of the home. Leather's durability makes it a cost-effective texture to use in the home. Team it with opposites, such as wool and silk, to make the most of its solidity and chunkiness. Try using it on furniture or as an unexpected trim on soft furnishings.

LIMESTONE

Use limestone to introduce an array of subtle colours into your home. Tough and hardwearing, it is perfect for floors and bathroom

surfaces, or anywhere that is likely to take some knocks. It can also be used in small quantities elsewhere – such as for a runner on a table. Combine stone with wood to bring out the textures in both, especially in flooring.

LINEN

This fabric is one of my personal favourites, which I use in my own collections. Linen is a natural fabric and comes in a wide choice of subtle colours and finishes. It is highly versatile and is the perfect neutral on which to add other textures. It looks great teamed with mohair.

LINEN & CALICO (MUSLIN)

These fabrics make an excellent combination and I have now teamed linen and calico in my own collection. They provide a neutral, unintrusive backdrop to a scheme and are also appealing in their own

right. Try combining linen throws with calico cushions for textural contrast and interest.

MOHAIR

One of the most tactile fabrics, mohair also comes in an array of colours. Use it for curtains rather than soft furnishings though, as it does not wear as well as cashmere.

Partner it with an opposite – linen or calico (muslin), perhaps – for maximum textural impact.

MOSAICS

These tiny tiles can make a large impact and you do not need many to make a difference. Just a line of them to form a border detail is often enough to lift a whole bathroom, or even a cloakroom. There are many colours and designs available, including metallic and mirror effects.

NATURAL FLOOR COVERINGS

Sisal, jute, seagrass, coir and other naturals continue to grow in popularity and are beginning to oust conventional carpet from the limelight. They are available in a choice of colours and are good-looking in their own right, as well as providing the perfect backdrop for rugs and runners.

PAINT

This is the most traditional of finishes available, but it is still one of the most widely used. Paint is not simply about flat wall colour – it can now be used to bring texture to a variety of surfaces in the home. Colour is now not necessarily a paint's main characteristic. Metallic finishes and glosses have also become very popular.

PEBBLES

There are few things in life more pleasing to the fingers than the round, smooth contours of pebbles. Full of subtle colours and variations of tone, pebbles are among the most beautiful of natural objects – use them symmetrically, as they do in the Far East, to make a striking focal point within a room.

RATTAN

Although traditionally associated with conservatory and garden furniture, rattan takes on a new relevance when teamed with other materials, such as metal. It can often be found on oriental furniture, the clean lines and natural simplicity of which I find perfect for my schemes.

RIBBON

Ribbon is no longer confined to being used as a trim – although it is one way of introducing it into a room. It is now possible to buy fabrics that are woven streams of ribbon in glorious colours. Ribbon is available in many widths and finishes.

SATIN

One of the most sensuous fabrics available, satin's smoothness is unsurpassed. Use it to trim bedspreads, pillows and even curtains. It looks most effective when the light catches it or the wind blows across it. Team it with something rough, such as tweed or undyed linen.

SCRIM

Scrim is the upholstery fabric that is used for backing sofas and chairs, so everyone has some, but it is rarely seen. I have made it one of my signatures by using it as much as possible, on banners, runners and blinds. It is not always easy to work, but it is cheap and exciting to use.

SHEERS & VOILES

The role traditionally played by sheer curtains has been taken to new heights by the wide array of modern fabrics. They are no longer used merely to ensure privacy but are now teamed with a range of other materials for greater textural impact. Their translucent qualities make them particularly attractive as they add a light, airy feel to a room. They come in a wide choice of colours.

SILK

Traditionally the most luxurious and covetable of fabrics, silk still has a huge relevance in design today. This is partly because of the wonderful colours it comes in, but also its feel – rough and slubby or smooth and soft. Think of unusual ways to use silk – it works with just about anything.

SPECIAL PLASTER FINISHES

Texture need not be limited to furnishings. Textured wall surfaces have a highly tactile feel and have become increasingly popular as people realize their full potential for extending the boundaries of design. Plaster can be used in a variety of imaginative ways – try using it to mimic the appearance of suede. It is also an effective alternative to using traditional paint finishes.

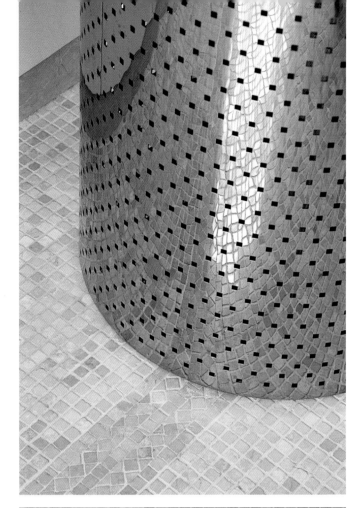

STAINLESS STEEL

Once used purely in industrial settings, stainless steel is now well integrated into the home. It adds a modern feel to a room. It is best suited to kitchens or bathrooms as a tough, durable worksurface. Alternatively, one can use it more creatively as a panel on a wenge table, a border around a floor or as a wall panel in a kitchen.

SUEDE

Suede is tough and durable, but has a softness that makes it very desirable. Use it with more feminine fabrics, such as silk or satin, to focus the attention on its textural character.

TAFFETA

Part of the appeal of taffeta is the wonderful way it falls – its stiffness allows you to mould it into the shape you want. Its crunchiness is almost addictive. The play of light on its surface is exquisite, especially on jewel-like colours, making it an excellent choice for glamorous schemes.

VELLUM

The opaque nature of this paper-like substance makes it the perfect foil to atmospheric lighting. When teamed with a dark, matt surface, such as wenge, its striking semi-transluscent quality has even

greater impact. It is ideal for screens or lampshades, but can also be used to cover a variety of furniture surfaces.

VELVET

One of the most tactile of fabrics – velvet constantly invites you to stroke it. It is ideal for places where you want to feel comforted and cocooned. The nature of the fabric brings a completely unique character and depth to colour.

WENGE

This wood has become one of my signatures – nearly every interior shown here has a piece of furniture in wenge. Originating from the Awong tree on the African continent, it was originally used for floors and staircases but is now being used to create stark, sculptural furniture. Its dark surface makes it the ideal canvas on which to introduce other textures. It also brings an exotic edge to a scheme.

WOOD

The most traditional of furniture and flooring materials, yet designers continue to use it to extend the boundaries. Combining wood with less obvious materials – such as stainless steel or stone – gives it a contemporary twist. Use it to add warmth to a scheme.

WOOL

The matt feel and the brilliant choice of colours combine to make wool a winning ingredient in every home. It works with everything, but it looks especially wonderful teamed with silks, satins and other shiny fabrics. Try using it for cushions, throws, upholstery, and at windows, as well as in places where a warm texture is needed. Wool is a relatively inexpensive material and is an important staple of my texture boards.

INTERIORS

INTRODUCTION

Using texture is all about learning to look at interiors in a new way. Having shown the variety of influences that inspire textural choices and the elements needed for a successful scheme, the next step is to look at the specifics of certain rooms. This half of the book is devoted to rooms that I have designed myself, ones where texture has been an essential component of the result. These examples are grouped together so it is possible to look at various different hallways, for example, or living rooms or bathrooms. The finished result is shown, while alongside I explain my design philosophy and the ingredients needed to build up texture to create both physical comfort and visual excitement.

I hope the examples I have chosen will make you feel confident enough to tackle design and decoration using texture in your own home. Don't feel disheartened if you may not be able to achieve the complete look immediately – texture is something that can be introduced slowly. In fact the mistake made so often with decoration is to rush through it in order to get the job done. It is better to leave yourself plenty of empty spaces that can be filled after you have had the chance to think carefully about what you want, rather than cluttering up every available surface. I hope you find plenty of ideas for small changes that can easily be replicated in your home. Begin to build up your own portfolio of ideas and inspirations, and before long you will be amazed at how fertile and productive your own creative thoughts have become.

ABOVE TOP

These wrought iron-and-crystal lights create a futuristic feel.

ABOVE BOTTOM

Ribbon-and-silk curtains bring semi-transparency to a room. The linen chair covers have a silk square detail.

RIGHT

This serene dining room has a simple wenge table and cabinet and linen-covered chairs. A pair of elegant freestanding lights by Mark Brazier-Jones cast magical shadows on the untextured walls.

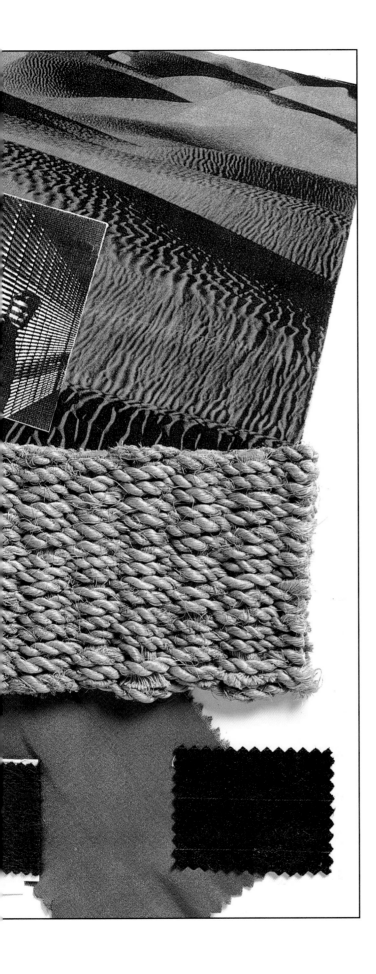

TEXTURE BOARDS

If you are starting to design a room from scratch, then it makes sense to marshal your random ideas into some sort of order. The best way of doing this is to put them down on paper, and this is where storyboards come in.

Designers use storyboards to show clients exactly what they are thinking. They include samples and photographs of the sorts of fabrics, colours and furniture that will make up the scheme, and also sketches and magazine cutouts that sum up the atmosphere of the proposed room. These boards take their name from the notion that good design does indeed tell some sort of story. Their advantages are three-fold: first, they give a three-dimensional format to a set of ideas and themes. Second, they allow you to see how different elements – such as upholstery fabric and moulding paint colour – will work together. Third, they show where inspiration has come from.

Storyboards often start with just one glorious image, from which the rest of the design inspiration follows. It could be an art exhibition catalogue, a glossy fashion photograph, a postcard from an exotic location – absolutely anything that serves to spark off a whole new set of ideas. Sometimes the starting point comes from me, but often it comes from the client, who might have collected ideas from magazines. One thing leads to another and soon the board will be covered with all sorts of images that support the first one.

Not surprisingly, many of my storyboards are in fact 'texture boards'. Texture is so central to my work that it often

LEFT

This texture board shows the inspiration for my dining room. Among my influences were the patterns the wind makes in the desert and the shape of silhouettes against the sky. I like to begin with the tactile element of fabrics – they immediately create a certain ambience. Silk, linen and ribbon all play a part. Symmetry was also an integral part of the design, and the two specially commissioned lights set the mood of the room early on.

dominates, even at this stage. I might begin with a picture of a dry riverbed, an embroidered couture dress, or an architectural landmark. Something in the surface will have excited my interest – the way light falls across it, or the mood it suggests. Then, from there, I start to build around it – finding other textures that either mirror it or contrast with it. It is likely that I already have certain materials in mind, suggested by the source of inspiration: ice might have already become satin in my imagination, or earth suede. As I play with the images on the board, detailing often becomes clearer – what to use for trimming the cushions perhaps, or which type of buttons to use on the upholstery.

At this stage the specifics are added: particular fabrics, carpets, paints, furniture or any other components that fit into the overall look. When you are putting your own storyboards together, you might find it helpful to write brief notes around pictures or samples. Bear in mind, too, that you can include things on the board that are out of your budget, – if they are useful in guiding you towards the right look.

Once you have completed your texture board – and it might take days or weeks before you are really happy with the finished result – put it in a prominent place and live with it for a while. You can still move, remove or add things at this stage. Now order larger pieces of the samples and pin them up around the room. Still happy? Then it is time for your story to become reality.

RIGHT

The texture board shown here was one I used when designing my own bedroom. Snow-falls and frozen surfaces were at the forefront of my mind and these led me towards materials like marble and plaster.

The satin-trimmed cashmere bedspread was inspired by soft flurries of snow edged with ice, an idea taken up in the satin-trimmed curtains. Other fabrics – hessian (burlap) and tweed – were chosen for their sense of earthiness.

NEUTRALS

As texture becomes more important in the home, colour becomes less so. One of the reasons neutral schemes have become so chic in recent years is that they take on a whole new dimension when they are used as a canvas for textural contrasts. A room furnished with different weaves, weights and finishes of a neutral fabric would be beautiful because of its simplicity. Add to this the subtle variations of colour within the neutral palette – whites to creams to stones to taupes – and it becomes clear that neutral does not mean boring.

By using barely-there colours, you draw attention towards texture instead. It could be that you start with rough unplastered walls and a white-washed knotty wooden floor. Now add generous, undyed calico (muslin) curtains, tweed upholstery, linen throws edged with fur, a metal table and a glass vase filled with white arum lilies. Everything is calm and restrained. Indeed, the appeal of such schemes is that you can return home from your frantic daily life and relax in an atmosphere so peaceful that it cocoons you from the pressures outside. Such rooms work because they combine spirituality with sensuality: the core of design thinking today.

Good lighting is an essential ingredient of neutral schemes – both natural and artificial – since, without it, textural surfaces will be flattened out. Cleanliness is also vital – these interiors are so simple that any grime or dirt will show. Think also about introducing scent – try to create an environment that appeals to as many of the senses as possible.

LEFT

Just one corner of a room can hold a wealth of textural interest. The limestone-and-iron coffee table contrasts beautifully with the vellum-covered box and basketweave Chinese trunks. Chenille has been used on the sofa, while the chairs have linen-and-chenille upholstery. Each ingredient – from the flooring to the dishes on the coffee table – has been selected with care, and as a textural companion to something else.

NEUTRALS

Draw your inspiration from the natural world – stones such as granite, limestone or slate; woods such as beech or sycamore; plants such as cacti, willow or wheat. Surround yourself with objects of natural beauty – a bowl of seashells perhaps, or a collection of shiny pebbles or the sculptural shapes of flint. Neutral interiors take on a Zen-like beauty because they are serene and uncluttered. They are calm and soothing in their simplicity. Not surprisingly, they are popular with followers of feng shui because it is thought they allow energy to flow freely around a room.

It is certainly true that neutrals appeal to people who value their spiritual health more than material possessions. Perhaps this is because the success of such rooms lies in recognizing the important things in life and surrounding yourself with them. Texture is central to this philosophy, because it focuses the mind on the object itself and the beauty inherent in it. Every object therefore has a value and is chosen for what it brings to that particular environment. This is quite different to conventional decorating where a confusion of furnishings and colours fight for attention and where some items may dominate. In the neutral scheme, no element is allowed to unbalance or overwhelm the others.

FAR LEFT
This striking limestone basin gives a sculptural quality to a neutral bathroom.

LEFT
Textural contrasts, like this velvet chair and bamboo ladder, make a strong statement in neutral rooms.

ABOVE
Fireplaces provide focal points within rooms, particularly in living areas. They don't have to be ornate or old, as this carved limestone one proves. Its strength comes from its inherent beauty and simplicity.

CREATING A MOOD

It is well documented that colour can alter mood, yet few people seem to make the connection between mood and texture. This is surprising when you consider what textures evoke in the mind. In some cases there is an obvious link: lingerie designers, for example, use lace, satin and silk to send out sensuous signals. You should take time thinking about the messages you want your home to give on your behalf. If you want guests to feel relaxed and at ease, then texture can help achieve this. If you want to live out a fantasy of glamour and romance, then use texture to make it become real. If you want to design a space that is stimulating and exciting, then you need texture to make it happen.

When first assessing the room you want to tackle, think about how you are going to use it, but also think about how you would like to feel. Let us start in the hallway. Here you want to feel your heart lift every time you walk in. Your home is your sanctuary and you want to feel embraced by it – safe from the outside world. It is also the first place that guests see when they visit, so you want it to signal positive messages about you and your home. Texturally, you can be bold – the design here should hold the interest and entice people inside.

Now imagine walking into the living room, thinking carefully about the transition from the hallway. The living room is the place in which you unwind, talk to friends, perhaps read, listen to music or watch television. It is important that you feel safe, comfortable and unthreatened in this space. You don't want guests to perch uncomfortably on the edge of their chairs – you want them to relax, put their feet up, sprawl on the floor. You want them to leave feeling that they have had a wonderful time. That means using textures that evoke feelings of warmth and security: velvet, chenille, suede, cashmere and fur all have that tactile quality that encourages people to snuggle down in them and let go of feelings of anxiety or stress.

The dining room, however, needs to bring out different character traits: you want guests to be alert, talkative, funny and energized. So the textures you choose should be those that stimulate rather than calm. Glass, metal, stone, wood,

LEFT

Start with cool summer elegance – this sumptuous look has been created with velvet chenille on the sofas, silk at the windows, and suede on the ottomans. The table is made from a distressed wooden base with a glass top.

ABOVE

Now the mood is warmed up for winter by using fabric. An African throw conceals the glass top, and red silk cushions with velvet bands are positioned for maximum impact on the understated upholstery fabric.

75

LEFT AND RIGHT

Just one material can have an enormous impact on a scheme as a whole. Here moleskin bedcovers are central to the bedroom's impact, but textural excitement has been introduced through straw cushions, feather-trimmed shawls and the wall-mounted African runner. With the removal of the runner, the headboard becomes a focal point.

ceramics and very neutral textiles, such as calico (muslin) and linen, create a stage on which the key players – you and your guests – can play their part. That is not to say that everything should be hard and sharp – this is a dining room, not a company board room – but textures should form a backdrop without intruding too obviously.

Kitchens are similar: they too demand that you feel awake and in control rather than mellow. Kitchens today are usually not just for cooking – they are the place where the family eats, the children do homework, the television is housed, or the home office is found. So you may want to create a completely different mood in the cooking and working end of the kitchen to the eating and talking part. Texture can help: use a soft rug or sisal mat to indicate the dining area and introduce fabric at the end of the room you want to eat in – this will immediately soften the hard lines of the kitchen furniture. And make use of lighting to dim down one area while bringing attention to another. It is something you have

probably already done instinctively: being aware of texture allows you to think about ways of accentuating these differences even more.

Bathrooms reflect a recent change of mood. Traditionally very clean, cold and clinical, bathrooms are now havens of sensuality that should envelop you completely. Floors, windows, furniture and lighting have all become softer: think of it as an extension of the bedroom rather than a room to be mentally paired off with the kitchen. You want your bathroom to be as tactile as possible, so choose ingredients that will make you feel pampered and treasured every time you step inside. Start small if that's what your budget allows – scented candles, huge fluffy towels, burning oils, a portable CD player, kinder lighting – these can make all the difference to how you feel when bathing.

From the bathroom, it is a short step to bed. Here you can let your imagination run riot. Bedrooms should be warm, cosy, sexy and deeply personal. They should be somewhere

LEFT AND RIGHT *Accessories are essential to finish off a scheme perfectly, but use a select few for maximum impact. Single-stem flowers in matching test-tube vases look sublimely chic. Look for ways of introducing accessories to change the tempo within a room. These purple runners over the plain linen chairs and satin bands laid over place settings lend a sense of glamour that is just perfect for evening entertaining.*

you can relax and unwind in, somewhere to be private. They share a lot of the same attributes as the living room, but can go one step further again. If you can, go for the most luxurious fabrics imaginable – cashmere, satin, silk, organza – whatever you personally adore. You can make these go a long way by partnering them with more modestly priced fabrics, such as cotton or linen. You should walk into your bedroom and feel joyous each time.

Of course there are other rooms in the house to consider as well – a guest room, perhaps, home office, conservatory, children's bedrooms – in these, too, you need to think about mood as well as function. Once you begin to analyse what is already happening, unplanned, with texture, you will start to see how easy it is to use it as a design tool. When you begin to trust your fingers as much as your eyes, you will be well on the way to mastering the art of texture.

HALLS & STAIRS

Your hall is not just a passageway through to the other rooms in the house. It is a room in its own right and deserves the same thought and attention to detail as your living room, kitchen, bedroom or bathroom.

Remember that you only have one chance to make an entrance. When people walk into your hall, it gives them an immediate message about you, your taste and what to expect from the rest of the house. You want to create a feeling of excitement and interest, not an immediate dampening of the spirit. Not that I approve of the notion that you decorate only with others in mind; this is your home and it should be decorated for you and your family, not for guests. But if you decorate the hall well you will feel your spirits rise every time you cross your own threshold.

When designing a hallway, try to take several points into consideration: the position of the front door, windows and staircase; whether you look through immediately into other rooms; and whether you want to create a room that stands alone or is part of a wider scheme unifying other spaces. If you want to, you can go a little crazy in the hall – this is one of the few areas where you can give priority to dramatic effects rather than function. So be as bold as you want to be and enjoy the reaction as people walk in.

The floor can play a key part. Stone and wood – or a combination of the two – are practical and attractive, and the

RIGHT
This tranquil hallway shows my signature Kelly Hoppen banners framing the doorway and leading the eye through to the room beyond. This space is ideal for displaying treasured pieces of art, such as this curvaceous bronze sculpture.

FAR RIGHT
Train your eye to see inspiration all around you – the graphic lines of fencing on a beach echo those found in stairways and banisters. The intricate patterns created by wood, sand and light offer a wealth of ideas for the home.

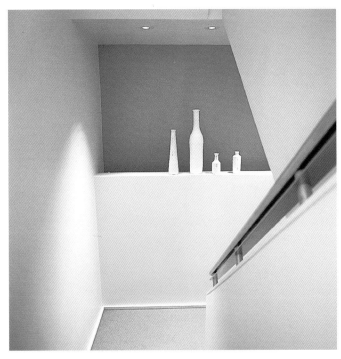

choice of colours and designs is limitless. As halls tend not to be large, an expensive floor surface might also be an option.

If you have a beautiful staircase, draw attention to it by having very little furniture. I like to underdress halls since they often have more impact when a little spartan. Console tables with tall lamps are not my style – I prefer to introduce more sculptural elements that have an immediate visual impact. Surfaces for keys and other essentials are important, but a simple shelf will often suffice.

Part of the enjoyment of entering a hall for the first time is the sensation of catching glimpses of other rooms. You can exploit natural curiosity to good advantage by thinking about where to lead the eye as someone walks in. Mirrors, pictures, runners and furniture can all play a part in the overall success of the scheme. Think of ways of giving more importance to doorways: fabric banners hung at each side, for example, lead the eye to the room beyond. They also give the opportunity to introduce another textural layer.

As with other rooms in the house, lighting is a crucial ingredient. Hallways should not be so brightly lit that guests are dazzled and left blinking when they enter; neither should they be so dim that your guests stumble over an umbrella stand. Stairs must be well lit for safety, but you should also be able to change the ambience of the lighting according to the season, time and occasion.

FAR LEFT TOP AND BOTTOM
Make use of otherwise forgotten spaces, such as landings halfway up the stairs. With the addition of shelves and spotlights, these can become ideal display areas for objects of beauty – such as these simple clay pots or a solemn bronze Buddha.

LEFT
The shape and form of staircase and banisters can be accentuated with clever use of bordered carpet. The black binding that edges this wool two-tone design brings a strong sense of geometry to the overall look.

HALLS & STAIRS

Part of the beauty of staircases – and another reason for choosing a hard floor – is the shadows they cast. Decorative banisters are one of the few ornamental designs that I love, because of the sculptural nature of their shape. Good lighting gives them the attention they deserve.

Once you have lighting, flooring and fabric in place, you can look at whether it is necessary to add more texture. Walls are often best kept plain, but you can accentuate rough against smooth, or matt against gloss with a few decorative objects carefully chosen for these qualities. Sculpture can be a successful addition to a hallway as it makes an immediate impact and appeals directly to the tactile sense. A well-proportioned hall can be similar to an art gallery – hard flooring, a minimum of furniture, good lighting, the feeling of people passing through – all these things conspire to create the ideal atmosphere for displaying art.

While the hallway itself will receive most notice, do not ignore landings or stairwells. Recessed areas halfway up stairs are often dark, neglected corners. Make these a feature with good lighting, shelving and objects of interest – perhaps a collection of some sort, a plinth with a sculpture, or a small library area. Landings should be thought about in the same way as the downstairs hall. They, too, are more than corridors leading to other rooms – decorate them to accentuate the feeling of unity within the home.

RIGHT
In my own hallway I have created a feeling of Zen-like serenity by keeping the room cool and minimalistic. Doorways have slim opaque panels of glass that are reminiscent of the slit windows found in castle battlements. A polished limestone floor complements the matt wall panels and elongated door handles. To add an edge to the scheme, a primitive-looking wooden chair has been chosen, while sculptural stone logans from David Champion accentuate the futuristic atmosphere.

Living rooms

The difference between designing a living room and merely revamping one lies in tackling function before starting decoration. So the first thing to consider is how you are going to use this room. Do you like to come home from work and slump in front of the television, put loud music on, pour yourself a drink, read the paper, talk all evening, eat on your lap, or catch up on work? You might do all of these things or none of them. But you must be honest with yourself and decide what your own priorities are for this room.

Once you have decided the functions you want from the room, you must look at the space you have and how best to use it. If you are lucky enough to have a large living room, you might consider whether you want to use it as one complete space or whether you want to create zones – perhaps one for listening to music in; one for studying in; one for sitting and talking in. You might also want to make these flexible enough that they can be easily merged together when necessary – at Christmas time, for example, when you might well want more sitting space.

The key to both function and space often lies in where you keep the television. A living room with a television has quite a different character to one without. The latter is by definition a gentler place – perhaps somewhere to talk to friends, listen to music and read. An easy solution if you are short of space is to put the television in the bedroom – it is a comfortable,

RIGHT

Your clothes send out signals about your personality, mood and how you feel about yourself. So it is with the home. The textures you choose can send out messages just as strongly as this sensuous dress by Hervé Leger.

FAR RIGHT

Immerse yourself in the most luxurious combinations of texture imaginable – this rich purple velvet sofa has been highlighted with cream suede cushions, which in turn have pearl buttons. This kind of attention to detail is breathtaking.

relaxing place, away from the core of the house. It also means that much of the unsightly paraphernalia associated with televisions, such as videos and remote controls, can also be removed from the key room.

If you want to keep the television in the living room, then position the furniture in such a way that the eye is not led to it the moment you walk in. There are few things worse than a half moon of seats arranged to face the box in the corner. It is not necessary to conceal today's attractive television sets, but if you do, make sure that you choose the cabinet with care – it should work in the room in its own right.

Lighting is absolutely crucial and should be seen as an investment worthy of a large part of the budget. Good lighting will lift any scheme to new heights and can make even the dullest of rooms come alive. When working with texture, it is an essential. But it must be installed at the beginning – cables, power sockets and switches cannot easily be installed at a later date. Major pieces of furniture, on the other hand, can be added over time.

To ensure the lighting is right, think back to function. You need lighting for day and for night; lighting for winter and for summer; lighting to read by and to eat by; low-level and high-level lighting; bright and dull lights; task lighting and ambient lighting. In fact, what you really need is the help of a lighting expert. It is not until you have seen their ingenious

FAR LEFT
Create a sculptural effect with a centre-piece, such as this chunky ammonite, set amid a line of single stems in test-tube vases. Think, too, about the way that you position furniture in a room – accentuating the look still further.

LEFT
Open shelves need not be cluttered with ornaments. Use them to focus attention on a few objects of beauty. Leaving space gives the impression the objects are floating within the room. Good lighting helps to reinforce this effect.

89

ways of bouncing light off walls and ceilings to create shadows and highlights that you grasp an inkling about the difference it makes in a room. Why invest in fabrics and flooring if they will be seen in flat, dull light? Good lighting will bring out the full potential of even the most inexpensive of rooms. You are setting the stage when you flick that switch – make sure it is going to have an impact.

Once I am happy that the space I am working with fits my client's brief for function – and that the lighting installed is perfect – then I start to consider the decorative side of the design. There are many myths about the design process, and the first of these is that you should work from the floor upwards. Traditionally, interior decorators found one beautiful carpet or rug that the rest of the scheme would be built around. However, fabrics are the starting point for me, because they offer the most textural possibilities. As soon as I have a feel for the people who live in a house, the location of the building, the views, the seasons, the architecture – then, instinctively, I begin to reach for fabrics that have the right connotations. The neutrals come first because rooms need a strong base; accents come later. I choose my clothes in the same way – neutrals with accents – a black suit accented by a floral scarf rather than a floral suit.

LEFT
Think consciously about contrasts when using textures together – here grey cashmere and purple satin cushions have a dynamic reaction.
RIGHT
Take the same cushions and place them on a silk-and-cotton sofa for an even greater impact.

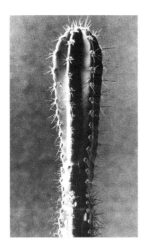

LEFT

Precisely arranged photographs echo the strong lines of this wenge coffee table.

ABOVE

Plants can add a layer of textural interest.

RIGHT

Borders highlight the space itself – like this taupe-edged carpet.

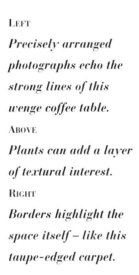

Some of the fabrics I use are the best available – exquisite cashmeres and taffetas that take your breath away when you handle them. But others are extremely inexpensive, for instance, upholstery scrim, which allows me to allocate some of the budget to splashing out on something luxurious, even if it is only to trim cushions. This is an important lesson when you are choosing furnishings for your own home: don't be led by your budget into looking at fabrics that are all of a similar price. Shop around so that within any scheme you can save money in one area and spend it lavishly in another.

Almost from the moment I first walk into a room, I carry in my head the image of what it will look like eventually.

Focal points are important here, and most living rooms benefit from having a fireplace of some description to build a scheme around. The fireplace itself should be worthy of attention: make something of it by dressing it in such a way that you can capture the attention even more. Light real fires in it if possible, and avoid the depressing cliché of a fireplace with nothing but a dusty bunch of dried flowers in it. An alternative for rooms without a fireplace is to invest in one large beautiful piece of furniture or work of art that will become the focal point. Consider carefully where it should go and how it will affect the positioning of the other furniture. The importance of focal points is another good reason for removing the television from the living room. Too often the television dominates because of its position – you need something else to focus the eye on.

It is usually not until this stage that I consider flooring. In a living room, for me, this means carpet. I like to create rooms that have such a relaxed atmosphere that guests are as happy to sit on the floor as on the sofa. That means the floor must be soft. Much as I love the look of wood or stone floors, I would rarely use them in the living room unless they were teamed with large and luxurious rugs. I also like to have big floor cushions as well as conventional armchairs for the same reason. A living room should be a comfortable place where you gather with friends and family to laugh, talk and unwind.

When considering furniture, scale is all-important. In my view it is better to buy large and have fewer pieces than to buy modest-sized designs. A huge coffee table, for example, has many advantages: you can sit on the floor and eat from it when feeling relaxed; guests always have somewhere to put a drink; books and magazines can be piled up on it; and it makes a bold statement within the scheme. Of course it should not be too big – you have to be able to walk around it comfortably, but you should go for the biggest you can. If you are concerned that a large piece of furniture will look too solid, then look at designs in glass or clear plastic – their transparency gives a sense of space. Over-scaling – as this sort of design philosophy is called – gives far more impact to

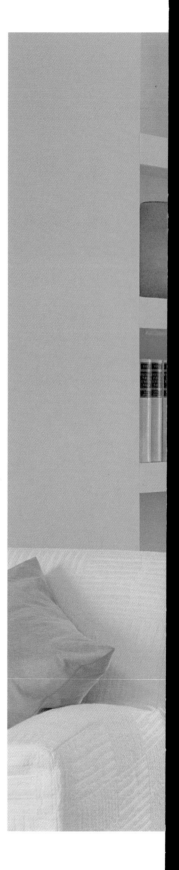

94

a room. Interestingly, even the smallest of rooms can look bigger if you fill them with just a few over-scaled pieces. Scaled-down furniture will draw attention to the fact that a room is meanly proportioned.

If you are designing your room yourself, you should learn to use a scale ruler. Draw a scaled plan of the room on graph paper and cut out scaled outlines of the furniture you are planning to use. It is the only way that you will know for sure that everything will fit in the way that you want it to – you will also know that you can physically get the furniture through the door and into the room.

The most important thing in living rooms is comfort. There is no point in having a to-die-for room if guests feel so ill at ease they perch awkwardly on the edge of the sofa. Fabrics that are soft to the touch comfort you and encourage you to relax, so choose upholstery fabrics with care. Personally, I prefer furniture with geometric shapes: curves and circles have never interested me as much as squares and lines. The furniture I choose tends to be strong in shape. And this is often accentuated by cushions, runners and banners that I then add to a room.

You might like to spare a thought for the changing seasons at this stage. Loose slipcovers for sofas and cushions are my favoured choice because they enable you to reflect in your furnishings the transition from airy, sunny days with windows left open to cold, rainy days that send you scurrying indoors

OPPOSITE AND ABOVE
The main seating area should invite guests to touch as well as to look – the soft ridges of this chenille-and-silk upholstery demand to be stroked, as does the vellum of the chest. Take pleasure, too, from introducing rough surfaces, such as this Chinese basketwork or carved chest.

97

LIVING ROOMS

for comfort. Taking down winter curtains and replacing them with light sheers also transforms the atmosphere of a room completely. The idea of winter-to-summer decoration used to be one that few people took seriously, but now it is becoming commonplace all over the Western world.

By this stage of designing a room, I have brought in layers of texture through lighting, flooring, furniture and soft furnishings. Now is the time to think about the walls. Plain walls are the perfect canvas for works of art, and it is always important to have some areas that are completely plain in order to throw more attention on those that are not.

It is for this same reason that I try to expel all needless clutter from living rooms – we fill enough other rooms with our flotsam and jetsam. Living rooms are for relaxation, and there is nothing calming about being surrounded by all manner of bits and pieces that are out of place. I like to keep

ABOVE

Hanging three-dimensional objects on the wall brings interest to a room – this line of masks has a sculptural quality and is another way of layering texture in unexpected ways.

RIGHT

Velvet is one of the most sensual and visually satisfying fabrics to bring into a room – here it has been used on its own and combined with linen for textural contrast.

98

CDs and other home entertainment essentials in the dinin
room rather than the living room, for example. All you real
need in your main living space is somewhere to sit, a surfa
on which to put a drink, and a place for your music syster
Banish all non-essentials to other places within your home

If that is easier said than done – if you have young childre
for example – then think carefully about storage. Wel
thought-out storage can have an astonishing impact on th
ambience of a room. It is often simply a case of making su
that everything you keep in this room has a place and that
is always put away there after use.

Don't rush to fill up every corner and surface. Just as pla
walls give impact to textured areas, so empty corners can pla
an important part in the success of a room. I think
is far better to live with too few things than too many.
is such an enjoyable feeling when you know you are goin
to buy something you really want, and it is just the opposi
when you feel you are drowning in possessions. Make som
much-needed breathing space, think about what you reall
desire, and only buy something when you know where it
going to go in the room.

Of course there are all sorts of additional elements you ca
bring into your living room. Scent is a wonderful way o
uplifting the senses and erasing that jaded feeling when yo
return home. Fresh flowers, burning oils, scented candles o
incense will emphasize the sensuous feel of the room – fo
sensuous it will be when you have chosen every texture an
surface with care.

LEFT
*Designing a successful
scheme is about
layering textures. This
sculptural table makes
the perfect display
area. Framing it at
each side are chenille-
covered chairs.*

*Their tactile qualities
are echoed at the
window with voile an
velvet curtains. Think
too, about the idea of
over-scaling within a
room – here, one
enormous vase has
great impact.*

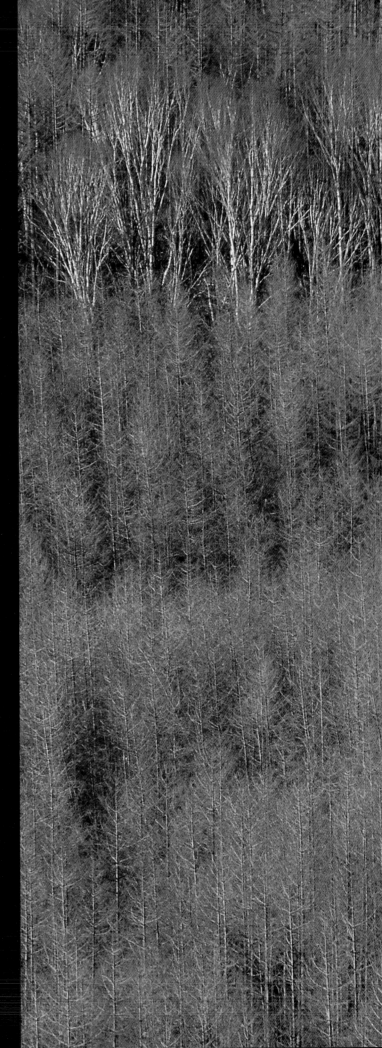

DINING ROOMS

Space is at a premium in most houses, so dining rooms often have to double as home offices, hobby centres, playrooms or display galleries for treasured objects. If they are used solely for dining, they are often not the only eating room – most people prefer to have a more informal eating area in the kitchen and keep the dining room for dinner parties and special occasions.

Because a dining room needs to be an adaptable space, you usually have to come up with a scheme that has an element of versatility. A dinner party demands that guests feel comfortable, yet alert enough to help the conversation sparkle. A family lunch on a Sunday, on the other hand, has quite a different feel to it and, because many of the guests may be young, practical issues such as easy-to-clean upholstery are often high on the agenda.

You should start by assessing the space itself. Sliding partitions can be used very effectively as a way of extending or minimizing space according to how many people you are entertaining. A dining room, for example, that links to the hall can be designed so that some of the hall area is borrowed as extra dining space when necessary. The same applies if your dining area is actually part of your major living space.

The dining room – like the hall – gives your guests an impression of you and your home. Eating, drinking, laughing, talking – our enjoyment is elevated by the ambience of our

RIGHT

A forest on a crisp autumn day offers a wealth of colour and texture. The outline of branches against the blur of foliage is a perfect example of hard edges against a soft backdrop. Furniture and fabrics can echo this effect.

FAR RIGHT

A classic combination – a simple wenge table with the contrasting texture of dining chairs upholstered in luxurious Alcantara suede. A plain vase of flowers highlights the simple, understated sophistication of this dining room.

By keeping a dining room very simple and chic, it can be dressed up or down as required. This room shows how little is needed once the core ingredients are in place. The elegant white china from Maryse Boxer completes the effect.

BELOW

Dining rooms are the perfect setting in which to display objects that you have collected. People have the chance to appreciate the beauty of the arrangements you create around a room – even something as simple as these white glass vases.

surroundings. Nobody should feel cold or uncomfortable when they are trying to relax in someone else's home.

Meals should be leisurely affairs, conducive to people sitting on and continuing conversation long after the plates have been cleared away. Soft lighting, appropriate music, not to mention delicious food and drink – these are the elements that make for successful entertaining. But well-thought-out décor puts a really special spin on the whole room.

The formula for designing a dining room lies not in one particular style, but will be influenced by many factors. The size of your family; the age range of your guests; how formally or informally you like to entertain; how often you are likely to use the dining room; what other purposes it is to be used for and whether it is to be used at night, by day, or both.

The size and aspect of the room are your starting points – then you need to think about what must go into the room. Write down a list of functions for the dining room and think about how these translate into the furniture you will need. Naturally, there will be a table and chairs, but there will also need to be storage of some description.

The table is the centrepiece of any dining room, but a beautiful – and expensive – table is not essential. It is how you dress the table that makes all the difference – sumptuous

FAR LEFT
My trademark Kelly Hoppen runner has been used to give emphasis to this silk-covered two-tone dining chair. Groups of wax-seal pictures framed in black give a sculptural quality to the walls, while the silk curtains emphasize the room's luxurious nature.

LEFT
Seen in its totality, this dining room is cool and elegant. The beautiful David Linley table at its centre is complemented by the silk-upholstered chairs and the long silk curtains.

tablecloths, elegant runners, linen napkins, brilliant glass, polished knives and forks, beautiful plates, elegant candlesticks – these are worth spending money on. The table itself could be made of chipboard. It is essential, however, to choose one that is the right size and shape for the room. It should always fit comfortably enough to allow you to walk around so that guests can be served easily; but whether it is round, square, rectangular or oval is entirely up to you.

Comfort is the key word when choosing dining chairs. Knees should never feel pinched between the seat and the table; backs should be well supported; arms should be at a comfortable height for eating. In spaces that are restricted,

chairs that can be stacked or folded out of the way are useful; but of these, only a few, such as the famous Arne Jacobsen Butterfly chair, are truly comfortable.

Some sort of sideboard is useful for storing dining room essentials – cutlery, china, glasses and CDs. It is also a practical surface for keeping extra bottles of wine, salad and side dishes until they are needed. A trolley has the same purpose and, being mobile, is also highly functional.

A dedicated dining room that is used only for relatively formal occasions is the ideal space for displaying art and other decorative objects. These are probably safer from accidents here than in other more heavily used areas of the house. They

DINING ROOMS

also make an attractive conversation point. Think carefully about how best to display them for maximum impact: well-lit open shelves are ideal, but remember both they and the things on them must be kept scrupulously clean at all times. You can focus attention on your collection even more by painting a different colour behind the items as a backdrop.

As well as choosing and positioning furniture, remember to spend time on lighting decisions. A sideboard might require brighter lighting than the rest of the room to provide you with a practical surface for serving food where you are not cast into shadow. At the table, guests need to be able to see what they are eating, but to feel that the lighting is relaxing and flattering to them as well. Pictures and art objects need to be seen at their best. This means that lighting must be as versatile as possible, both in where it is positioned and how it is controlled. Dimmer switches, lamps and candles can make all the difference to existing lighting, but if you are starting from scratch, allocate some of your budget for professional lighting advice.

Décor is the next decision. If you have chosen furniture with textural contrasts, continue the theme with flooring and windows. Walls can be left relatively plain, particularly if you have art on display. Hard floors are a good choice in the dining room, being easier to maintain than carpet. Options

FAR LEFT

Stone is a wonderful material to bring into a room – it has a raw beauty that suits today's interiors perfectly. This granite slab, for example, is full of the most wonderful patterns, colours and textures.

LEFT

There are few things that give greater satisfaction than commissioning furniture to your own specifications. Not only will you be investing in a unique piece for your home, but you can also stipulate practical additions. This wooden dining table has a granite inset, which, in addition to its decorative appeal, is the perfect place for standing hot serving dishes. The dining chairs have corduroy covers with linen throws placed over the backs. These can be removed for cleaning or replaced for a different look.

now available include wood, stone, ceramic and metal, so the time has never been better to invest in something exceptional. However, if both the flooring and furniture are hard, then you should look for ways of introducing softness – perhaps by hanging sumptuous fabric at the windows or going over the top when dressing the table for dinner. I love to cover dining room walls in fabric where possible – Alcantara suede, silk, linen, wool, velvet, leather – these textiles immediately bring a sense of glamour and excitement to a dining room. But I don't allow style decisions to override functional matters – if you do have young children eating regularly in the dining room, you would do better to choose easy-to-maintain materials.

When considering your windows, you might want to have the option of screening them off at night to cocoon yourself from the outside world or letting the sun stream in during a summer lunch. Choose from floaty sheers, cosy chenilles, heavy linens, exotic silks and so on to find the combination you like best. I like to have an element of textural contrast

FAR LEFT
A dining room gives you the opportunity to be a little braver than usual. This aerial view gives the full impact of a dramatic dining table setting – the cloth is made from red velvet with blue and white wool runners criss-crossed over it. Chairs are upholstered in a woven material that gives them a very rough feel. The pair of moss balls at the centre of the table punctuate the flag-style design perfectly. The visual impact of the room comes from the juxtaposition of texture and shape – the curve of the chairs contrasts beautifully with the stark linear look of the table itself.

LEFT
These functional stainless steel place mats add a striking futuristic touch to the room. Their shininess is emphasized by the dark matt surface of the wenge side table.

DINING ROOMS

when dressing windows – a rough, tweedy blind, for example, could be framed by crunchy taffeta curtains.

Finally, bring in all the accessories that give a scheme its final flourish – mirrors, candles, decorative objects – to create a sense of layering within the room. Again, think about texture when you are choosing these, and position them against other surfaces in such a way as to draw the eye.

These same rules apply when designing a dining area that is linked strongly to the garden – perhaps in a conservatory or summerhouse. Eating outside somehow heightens the enjoyment of the whole process. You do, however, need some privacy, so choose the location carefully.

Comfort is again the key. Many people make the mistake of building a conservatory in a too-sunny position so that temperatures rise at an alarming rate. The secret is to design with all-year temperatures in mind – include heating, ventilation and lighting in the initial design, and make sure that it has blinds to block out the most fiery of suns.

Don't stint on tableware and glasses – the more luxurious they are, the more special it feels to eat outside, or nearly outside. You can even create a winter/summer look by changing chair covers, table linen and dinnerware. To accentuate the cosiness in winter, put a rug on the floor and hang thick curtains over the summer blinds – you could enjoy Christmas dinner here as much as a summer soirée.

RIGHT
Conservatory dining rooms should always have a feel of being a part of the outdoors as well as of the home. Here a driftwood table, steel chairs and tin pots of flowers make a delightful combination of rough with smooth, elaborate with simple.

FAR RIGHT
There are some materials available that seem as happy outside the house as inside, such as very rough linen, rattan or bamboo. Use these as transitional materials to help mark the boundaries between indoors and outdoors.

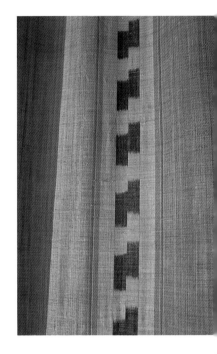

KITCHENS

In recent years, kitchens have become the very core of the home. No longer restricted to a being merely a room in which to cook, they are now just as likely to be used as a second living room, dining room, home office or television room. So the first task is to draw up a list of the functions you want the room to fulfil. The larger the space, the more versatility there is in the way you can break it down into zones. An important question when planning a kitchen is to consider whether there might be the possibility of extending it, perhaps by knocking into an adjacent utility room or cloakroom. Any structural alterations you undertake will be worthwhile if the result is some sort of eating zone within the kitchen.

Given the option, most families like to have two dining rooms – a separate dining room for formal dinners and special occasions; and a more relaxed dining area within the kitchen so they can chat as they prepare and serve food.

You also have to consider the people within the house. With small children, safety is a priority – as is easy maintenance of the materials you use. With older children, bear in mind they need somewhere to get together with their friends, so try to include a seating area in the kitchen if there is no other room where they can congregate to talk.

Careful ergonomic planning of a kitchen is essential. Calling on the professional services of a designer will always be well rewarded. Most contemporary kitchen design is based on

RIGHT

This view of the state-of-the-art Guggenheim museum in Bilbao, designed by Frank Gehry, shows the organic forms used by today's architects and designers. The remarkable use of these materials can inspire your own home.

FAR RIGHT

Stainless steel adds ultimate kitchen chic, but it will need careful maintenance in order to keep its non-scratch gloss. Here a wooden worksurface makes the ideal contrast to the metal – wood and steel work together to create modern sophistication.

114

KITCHENS

This sleek dining zone displays a wealth of textural play. The wenge table has my signature Kelly Hoppen stainless steel runner inset down the centre, and the limestone floor sets off this combination of materials beautifully. Arne Jacobsen chairs add more gloss.

the principle of a work triangle: this links the three main cooking activities – food storage, food preparation (including access to water), and cooking. Through traffic should be kept clear of the work triangle, particularly the area between the cooking appliances and the sink.

Traditionally, the kitchen has been a hard environment, without softening elements. In part, this is because of practicality – hygienic worksurfaces and wipe-down cupboard fronts are naturally desirable. Another factor has been most designers' appreciation of a streamlined look. Personally, I prefer the aesthetics of modern kitchens to the old-fashioned type, but if clients do prefer a more traditional look, I compromise by putting a twist in the scheme. For example, I might have a wenge or oak worksurface banded by stainless steel, or a laminate one teamed with granite. Modern does not necessarily mean clinical – but it does mean never sacrificing function to style.

Ease of maintenance is very important. All surfaces and materials must be resistant to water, steam, grease and smells, as well as being easy to clean. We all lead busy and stressful lives, so cutting down on maintenance improves the quality of our day-to-day life. For that reason, I would avoid black

ABOVE

A stainless steel sink set into a dark wooden worksurface is nothing new, but the sculptural quality of this design set into the wenge counter creates a fresh dimension. White vases in clay and wood continue the tactile theme while echoing the shapes around them.

kitchens as they show every mark. And if someone does want stainless steel – a favourite of mine – I will advise them that it does need careful looking after. with regular treatments of baby oil. Solid wood also demands regular attention and the occasional coating of tung oil.

The kitchen is not the place in which to be too fashion conscious. It is too expensive a room to change every couple of years. so it is better to go for something very simple. made of beautiful durable materials. which will age with grace.

Once you have a plan to work to. you must set about the task of choosing the materials. Texture accentuates mood. so if you want a look that is warm and comfortable. wood is a great option. If you prefer something cool and sophisticated. you might choose a laminate or metal. Materials should not necessarily be restricted to just one choice. With the recent trend for free-standing kitchens. it has become acceptable to put different pieces of kitchen furniture together for an interesting and eclectic look.

Worksurfaces are the next consideration. Laminates are the most widely used, being versatile and relatively inexpensive, but you might have a budget that could include ceramic. mosaic tiles. hardwood. slate. granite or terrazzo. Stainless steel is increasingly popular and looks its best when teamed with slabs of granite or slate.

Kitchen sinks were. at one time. nearly always stainless steel – now they come in ceramics. stone and even wood. Textural choice has never been more exciting. so explore all the options before deciding which one is right for you.

You should also spend time making sure the lighting is as good as possible. Each of the areas within the work triangle

LEFT
For those who favour a more traditional style. this warm cherrywood finish in a classic. unfussy design is an attractive option. The wood has been given more of an edge by combining it with a black granite slab set into the dining zone surface and glossy black laminate chairs.

needs its own task lighting – you should not be cast into shadow when working. A dining or sitting area needs ambient lighting to distinguish it from the rest of the room and to give it a relaxing atmosphere.

Much of the wall space is covered either with furniture – the wall units – or with accessories such as utensil racks, and so it is best to keep the walls relatively plain. But floors offer an opportunity for bringing in textural contrast. There are now so many options available – from metal, wood, stone and ceramic to rubber, vinyl and cork. Choose the finish for your cabinets and worksurface first – remembering that you can mix and match these – then try to find a floor that contrasts with the surfaces you have chosen.

You can use texture to accentuate the different zones within the kitchen. A dining area, for example, might have a rug on the floor and some sort of fabric detail to soften the atmosphere and separate it from the more practical cooking area. Screens are one way of doing this, and can be used to create an intimate cocoon when you want to introduce a more seductive tone. Fabric is not restricted to window use – you might have banners hanging down to frame the table, or choose to upholster the chairs, or place a straight line of cushions along a bench. You can still set the table in quite

LEFT ABOVE AND BELOW
Design today means breaking down traditional boundaries and having the confidence to team different materials together – as with this wood and granite worksurface, with inset stainless steel bin. It achieves both a functional purpose and an aesthetic one.

RIGHT
Colour can be used to highlight contrasts between the different design elements contained within a room – here burnt orange laminate is an effective foil to the stainless steel finish. The black gloss of the worksurface becomes a frame to unify these two surfaces.

a traditional way, so that you create a special atmosphere even though you are in the kitchen.

If you have French doors leading outside, then you do not need to dress the windows at all. Instead find ways of drawing attention to the outside, so that the kitchen feels as if it is spilling into the outdoors. If you do need privacy, louvred blinds or sandblasted glass are ideal choices.

Think about the extras, too – such as piping music through from your hi-fi system to speakers in the kitchen. The aim is that you should feel your mood relaxing as you move away from the cooking area and take your seat at the table. This applies to any seating area you might design in the kitchen. The mistake that many people make is to only take one view of each zone. They often stand in the centre of the cooking area looking at the dining or seating zone to see whether it works visually. You must also sit in the other zones and ensure that the view into the core of the kitchen is as pleasing.

Accessories also have a part to play in textural terms – willow baskets, ceramic pots, stainless steel gadgets – any of these can take on a significance when juxtaposed with another contrasting texture. The kitchen is ultimately a functional place, but there is still room to experiment with various components until you feel a glow of aesthetic satisfaction.

FAR LEFT
A granite work suface makes a strong visual and textural statement within a room. Here it has been teamed with cherrywood for maximum impact. The stainless steel hood and chairs bring in a modern linear element and a glossy dimension that set off the other materials perfectly.

LEFT
See how the same sorts of colours and textural contrasts are brought together in the natural world. These lichen-covered rocks share the same striking visual qualities as granite does with cherrywood, while the shininess of steel can be found in their reflections when wet.

Bedrooms & Dressing rooms

If there is one room you should design with your own needs in mind, it is the bedroom. You should feel that you can shut the door behind you at the end of the day and be safe, comfortable and shielded from worries. It is in the bedroom that you shed the stresses of the day and so you should be surrounded with things that give you pleasure. It is also the most personal place in the house, so you should always look forward to spending time here.

Too many people skimp on bedroom décor, perhaps thinking it is not as important as some other rooms because no one else will see it. However, I think the opposite is true. If you value yourself, you need somewhere that makes you feel really pampered and special.

It might not be the case that you use the bedroom only for sleeping: perhaps it is a study, a television room or a dressing room as well. In other words, the chances are that it functions not as one room but three or four. Consider too who else makes use of it. Is it only yours or do you share it with a partner? Do you have children or pets who like to climb into bed with you? Do you use it only at night or do you like to spend time in bed during the day? You need answers to all these questions before thinking about style or decoration.

If you can separate an area as a dressing room, it will make a big difference to the bedroom itself. So many master bedrooms become centres of chaos, as clothes, shoes, belts

RIGHT

Ornamentation for its own sake is often considered pointless in today's interiors, but the nickel detailing on this wooden chest brings an unusual tactile element into this bedroom. Other surfaces are kept plain to highlight it.

FAR RIGHT

The bed has been designed to look as soft and floaty as possible against the dramatic edge of the wenge cabinet. Upholstered in plain cotton, it has been draped in voile like a bride's wedding veil. A silk cushion and wool rug add contrast.

This bedroom has been layered with texture to become a haven of sensuality: combinations of both cashmere and linen with satin have been used for the bedcover and cushions; coarse linen with satin trims for the curtains; and goat vellum for the low console table.

RIGHT
Vellum wall panels set the mood for this sophisticated sitting area within a bedroom. The suede and oak ottoman, cashmere-covered sofa and wool carpet are soft and warm, while the lights are shiny and hard.

and underwear spill out on to the floor. It is important that everything you possess has a home within the room. By setting aside one area for clothes storage, you can concentrate on making the sleeping and relaxing space as sensual and calming as possible.

Begin then by assessing the space you have and whether it can be improved on architecturally. You don't necessarily need a large bedroom, so perhaps you should choose the room with the best view or the prettiest moulding. There might only be one furniture layout that is going to work, but think laterally in case you are missing another possibility.

Lighting is one of the first things that needs careful consideration. You can alter the whole mood of a room with a flick of a switch, so go for maximum control with dimmer switches and a really versatile lighting scheme. As with other rooms, you have to combine effective task lighting with ambient lighting. Task lighting is needed for specific activities, such as reading or applying make-up. Ambient lighting should be sensual, soft and flattering, so that you feel at your best when relaxing in bed.

However, you should also make the most of natural light – particularly first thing in the morning. Waking up in a room

LEFT

If possible, dressing rooms should be clean, elegant places where you can dress in an atmosphere of serenity. In practical terms, it is also a good idea to have somewhere to sit, rest suitcases or lay out clothes. Here light-coloured sycamore floor-to-ceiling storage sets the tone, as does an ornate glass chandelier. The day bed and ottoman are both upholstered in leather, which contrasts with their nickel bases and complements the coolness of the limestone-and-marble floor.

RIGHT

Accentuate the feeling of luxury within a bedroom or dressing room with a sumptuous wash basin – as with this beaten silver design set into a marble surface.

flooded with sunlight on a warm morning is the most positive start to the day. Soft voile curtains or unlined fabrics provide privacy while letting light in. Team them with thick tweed blinds for use when the days grow colder and shorter. The textural contrast of these fabrics is also effective – rough with smooth, opaque with sheer.

Increase the sense of being in a sanctuary in your bedroom through music. Consider connecting bedroom speakers to your main hi-fi system or buying a CD player solely for use there. I also like to have televisions in bedrooms, not only because it takes them out of the main living space where they are intrusive, but because watching television in bed is very comfortable and increases the sense that this is your own space, a place where you can do as you like.

The centrepiece of the bedroom is, of course, the bed. It must be as comfortable as possible – you spend roughly a third of your life here, so do not choose one that is too soft, too hard or too lumpy. Good health demands a full night's sleep, so you owe it to yourself to buy the best bed you can.

RIGHT

If you have a master bedroom large enough, design it around zones, as you would with other key rooms. Here the main sleeping area is central to the scheme, but there are also subsidiary seating and desk corners. The chairs have been upholstered in silk to complement the bedspread in piqué and silk. Curtains are a combination of cotton damask with silk. Colours, patterns and textures have been used to unify the scheme.

Choice of style in the bedroom is a very personal decision, but as with the dining room, it is the dressing up of the centrepiece that makes for a successful scheme. Four-poster beds are perennially popular, and today they can be dressed to look contemporary rather than traditional. Quilts have their place, but, if you want to feel pampered each night, nothing works so well as crisp linen sheets, soft lambswool blankets and delicate satin-trimmed cashmere throws. To give the bed even more significance, make the headboard as tall as possible. This has the effect of anchoring it to the room and making a strong visual design statement. By keeping the rest of the room relatively plain, attention is focused again on the bed itself.

The only other pieces of bedroom furniture you should incorporate are bedside tables, a dressing table and at least one chair. Bedside tables are for all those small, but essential, objects – reading lamp, books, telephone, water. Choose ones as large as possible, or your bits and pieces will end up using floor space as well. Every woman should have a dressing table – a space sacred to her where she can do her make-up, apply facial creams, dry her hair and generally pamper herself. If you cannot find a dressing table you like, customize an existing piece of furniture, such as a console table, then just add a free-standing mirror. Chairs are a must in a bedroom because you need somewhere to throw down the day's clothes, and they also accentuate the feeling that the bedroom is another living room.

Once you have decided on the layout of the room and incorporated the essentials, including lighting, you need to put your mind to décor. A bedroom ceiling is likely to be seen

Door surfaces can be used to bring together luxurious combinations of texture – as with this mahogany, brass and suede example.

ABOVE
Using blinds to screen off areas can work perfectly; particularly if you pay attention to the details, such as this exquisite tassel.

131

more than any other, so you could make a feature of it if you wish – perhaps by having some special light effect that casts patterns of shadow and light across the ceiling. Walls can be left fairly plain, particularly if you are planning to hang artwork on them. Floors, on the other hand, should be as soft as possible. A bedroom carpet is not subjected to as much wear and tear as one in the living room, so it isn't necessary to buy the highest quality – but do go for the most tactile option within your budget.

Tactile is the key word in the bedroom. Bedding, throws, upholstery, carpet, curtains – you can throw caution to the wind when choosing design elements for the bedroom. Colours can be kept muted, calming and peaceful – but textures should be rioting for attention. Increase the feeling of sensuality with fresh flowers, candles, large mirrors and intoxicating scents. And if you are lucky enough to have an open fire in the bedroom, then use it. Nothing could be more sensual than the smell, sound and warmth of a burning fire.

You must maintain your bedroom well though, otherwise the atmosphere will be spoilt. This is the main argument for moving clothes and accessories outside the bedroom domain completely: separate dressing rooms are a must if you have the space. If possible, keep yours separate from your partner's. For some men a dressing room becomes a sacred place – akin

LEFT
The starting point of this sophisticated scheme was the fake pigskin headboard – the luxurious tone was then accentuated with the mohair and satin bedcover and cashmere cushions with chrome buttons. Dark bedside tables anchor the whole scheme.

RIGHT ABOVE
The combination of wenge and pigskin continues with the dressing table and stool. Satin curtains are hung next to a coarse linen blind.
RIGHT BELOW
A line of three dark wooden balls makes a strong visual statement in a room.

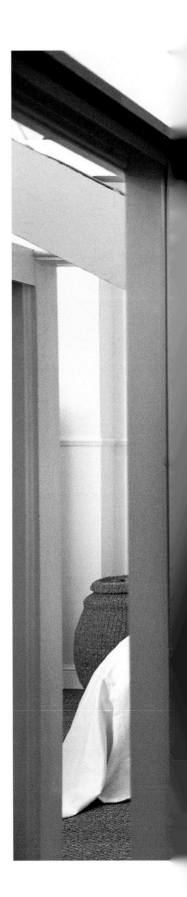

to a study. For a woman, it is a way of taking control of an area that too easily slips into anarchy. One of the joys of dressing rooms is that you can furnish them in a very utilitarian way for maximum economy of space. The most important consideration is to make sure you have enough hanging and shelf space, and that there is the potential to increase one or the other when needed. Whereas bedroom furniture has to be chosen to complement an overall scheme, dressing rooms are more likely to be designed around built-in, floor-to-ceiling cupboards with dividers between the various sections. There should always be a bench or chair on which to pack – luggage can be stored on high-level shelves. In terms of décor, you can have great fun because the space is usually so small and private. Outrageous schemes work here – cover doors with suede or gingham perhaps, then finally trim them in brass.

Once you have your own bedroom designed to perfection, you will probably want to take a fresh look at the others in your house. Children's rooms are always difficult – not least because their tastes and needs change so much as they grow. Unless you want to be trapped in a perpetual circle of redecoration, you should try to design not just with the current age of your child in mind, but also in how he or she will develop in the next three to four years. There are many

ABOVE
The pleasing lines of this simple wooden chair have been used to add a note of interest to the end of a bedroom. Furniture that you can see through in this way has both solid and non-solid qualities that gives it an impact when placed near a plain surface.

RIGHT
You must consider views into a room when designing a mezzanine bedroom such as this one. The design has to unify the space all around it, so try to keep it clean and uncluttered. This simple cotton bedcover sets the sophisticated tone of the room.

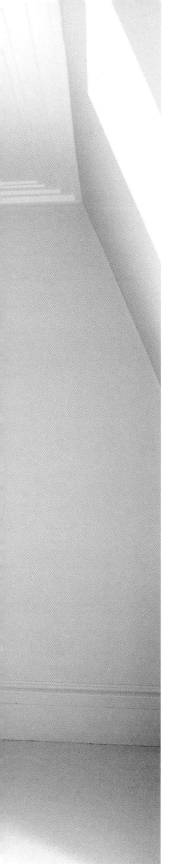

more practical considerations where children are concerned – floors, for example, should be hardwearing and easy to clean. Plenty of storage is needed, unless you are prepared to live with the anarchic look. Walls will be covered in posters, souvenirs and school artwork. The most successful strategy is to go for the simplest look – perhaps some sort of textured wall finish to contrast with a hard floor. Then allow the children to imprint their personality on their surroundings, and enjoy it rather than try to control it.

Teenagers should always be consulted on design – most have very firm ideas about what they want. You will find they are often drawn to tactile elements anyway – big squashy floor cushions, carpets they can lounge around on, exciting effects for both task and ambient lighting, comfortable throws and scatter cushions. Enjoy helping them put together a room that is contemporary enough to draw the admiration of their friends, while also becoming a comfortable sanctuary into which they can retreat to read or study.

The way you decorate a guest room is quite different from the way you might approach the decoration of your own room. To a certain extent, you could take as your inspiration or starting point a comfortable and intimate hotel you might have stayed in. You can use textures

FAR LEFT
This four-poster bed has been given a contemporary twist by being stripped down to its square shape. Everything else is neutral, so the furniture appears to be floating in space.

BELOW LEFT
Tear out evocative pictures for inspiration when designing your scheme as inspiration can come from the most unexpected images.

BELOW RIGHT
Accessories should be kept as simple as possible when the bed is the focal point.

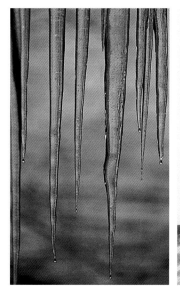

ABOVE

This moleskin and velvet bedcover and upholstered headboard provide a strong visual anchor in this attic bedroom.

RIGHT

Let your imagination run riot when it comes to detailing – here a sumptuous velvet bedspread is edged with carpet binding, while horn buttons have been sewn on to soft velvet cushions.

to create a calm, welcoming atmosphere for your guests. Sleeping in a different house is not always easy, and what all guests like is a comfortable bed, somewhere to hang their clothes, a chair and good lighting close to the bed. A few really personal touches can make all the difference – perhaps a few carefully selected paperback books, a bottle of mineral water, tissues, a clock, a vase of flowers. Always try to spend at least one night in the guest room yourself – only then will you have any idea how comfortable your guests are likely to feel.

The golden rule with bedrooms – no matter who they are for – is that they should engender a feeling of tranquillity and deep, fulfilling sleep. But the periods before you drop into sleep and when you wake up are crucial in making that happen. By giving thought to every element that is necessary, and choosing the best you can afford, you will create a bedroom that is truly in tune with your soul.

BATHROOMS

Bathrooms were for too long a neglected part of the house. Few people bothered to think much about making theirs a really special place. A coat of paint on the walls and some vinyl on the floor was about as much thought as went into decorating one – the thought being, I suppose, that too little time was spent in there to make good decoration really worth while. I would argue the opposite. I can't be the only person to enjoy the luxury of a leisurely bath; indeed, I have some of my best and most creative ideas in the bath.

But the challenge of decorating a bathroom lies in the fact that it has to cater for different moods. The feeling you have late at night when you are sleepy and want to get warm before climbing into bed is quite a different one to the early evening unwinding you may do before getting dressed up to go out. Similarly, you might want to dash around in the morning and have a quick shower before dropping in at the gym – which means you want to feel alert and energized, not massaged into drowsiness. Somehow you have to design a bathroom suited to each occasion.

Too often, bathrooms are small cramped spaces – perhaps added on to, or carved out of, existing bedrooms. So the first thing you need to consider is whether the room itself is suitable – whether it would be better to move the bathroom entirely into a larger space, or if there is a way of

RIGHT
Water rippling over pebbles creates the most magical effect, bringing out the colours of the stones and capturing light within the reflections. To understand how to use such inspiration, study the way each element complements the others.

FAR RIGHT
Stone with water has provided the inspiration here. An antique shallow stone bowl has been customized into a basin. The treated oak worksurface and glass accessories help highlight the textural theme of translucency against opacity.

making it larger or generally better proportioned through an architectural solution of some sort. They are expensive rooms to design, and sadly most of what you spend your money on will never be seen at all – the plumbing. Good plumbing is crucial to the success of this most sensual of rooms. You want to feel confident that each time you turn on the tap, hot water will be available – and that it won't suddenly run cold if someone has a shower elsewhere. Don't skimp on professional advice – there are too many complications and regulations to make it worth taking a risk.

Think about how you are going to use your bathroom. It might be for long leisurely soaks or speedy showers; just for you and your partner; for teenagers or for younger children; for guests; with a toilet here or elsewhere; as a laundry room; or whatever else seems appropriate. Then write down what this means in terms of fixtures, storage and accessories.

Designing with a particular person in mind will also give you clues as to style. Children's bathrooms are fun to do if you inject some fantasy into them, perhaps by taking a theme and continuing it through a panel, mural, wall decorations and accessories. Teenage bathrooms should be as functional and easy to maintain as possible – adolescents live life on the run, so it is unlikely they will appreciate your efforts at prettying up their environment. Guest bathrooms should be warm, comfortable and well equipped – make your friends

FAR LEFT
This classic roll-top bath design has been placed on treated oak plinths to accentuate its dominance for maximum impact.
LEFT
Natural sponges introduce a contrasting layer of texture.

ABOVE
The primitive, unfinished nature of this stone basin has been highlighted by the strong geometry of the shelves and mirror above it. This is a powerful combination of symmetry and organic form.

BATHROOMS

feel loved and pampered by adding little luxuries such as paperback books, flowers and aromatherapy oils.

Remember that a bathroom is a real room, not just an anteroom to a bedroom. The best bathrooms are those where you find sofas, chairs, linen chests or other pieces of furniture that make you feel as though you are bathing in a rather elegant living room. Anyway, as any parent knows, your child will need somewhere to sit when he or she arrives to ask a barrage of questions just as you are sinking into the water.

Bathroom fixtures can be very expensive, so it is important to get the layout of the room right. Tackle this the way you would the kitchen – with graph paper and scaled cut-outs, remembering to leave space for doors to open and essentials such as towel rails. Comfort is a top priority, so as well as good plumbing you must make sure that heating, ventilation and lighting are also taken care of. Condensation will build up if you don't make sure there is adequate ventilation. This is one room of the house that must be guaranteed to be warm – and to have hot, dry towels – at all times.

Lighting needs to be as versatile as possible, and again your first step must be to draw up a checklist of functions before finalizing it. Shaving, applying make-up, bathing, eyebrow plucking, toenail cutting – all these activities require good task lighting, so make sure you plan in advance where each one will take place. Spotlights or downlights are preferable to hanging fixtures on grounds of safety as well

LEFT
Bathrooms should be places where you can indulge yourself. Watching television in the bath, for example, seems rather decadent, but why not enjoy a glass of champagne, a favourite magazine or a phone chat as well?

Here the generous surround of the bath helps to define the space architecturally, while stainless steel, chrome and marble have been combined to create great luxury. Voile curtains soften the room's otherwise stark, cold lines.

145

RIGHT

Even in a relatively small space, you can gain visual satisfaction by combining different surfaces. Here, marble, sandblasted glass, stainless steel and mahogany create an elegant atmosphere.

RIGHT

Even in a relatively small space, you can gain visual satisfaction by combining different surfaces. Here, marble, sandblasted glass, stainless steel and mahogany create an elegant atmosphere.

FAR RIGHT

Use just one material in different finishes for textural contrast. The opaque glass on these bathroom cupboards partners the plain glass counter and the border of glass tiles around the floor.

as aesthetics. Lights around mirrors should be aimed into the face. Once you have the task lighting in place, you need to think about ambient lighting – preferably controlled by dimmers – so you can alter the mood from alert to comatose according to how you feel.

The bathtub is the focal point of the room – the equivalent of the fireplace in the living room, or the bed in the bedroom. Buy the biggest you can for the space you have – baths are so much more enjoyable if you can stretch out virtually full length. Whether you choose a traditional roll-top or a modern panelled style is entirely a matter of personal taste. But bear in mind the qualities of various bath materials – acrylic, for example, is generally warm, but cheaper versions chip easily and don't age well. Cast iron and vitreous enamel are more stable; marble looks opulent but is expensive; stainless steel is increasingly available, although until recently it was rarely

found outside of hospital bathrooms. If you want an unusual feature, such as a sunken bath, you should consult a structural engineer first. Think, too, about the bath surround – is this to be left plain or are you planning to panel it in some way? This is often the first textural decision you will make – wooden tongue-and-groove, for example, will immediately create a cosier atmosphere than that created by white tiles.

Washbasins, too, should be as large as the space permits. Generous-sized rims are useful for accommodating shampoos, facial rinses and the like. In my own bathroom, I have one custom-made from a shallow stone bowl – not only is this fabulous to look at and to touch, but it is also highly practical since I can stand bottles and make-up on it.

Toilets and bidets should be positioned for maximum comfort. Showers can be installed within a separate cubicle or incorporated into a separate shower area. Never cut corners

when choosing a shower – you must have a separate pump to keep the jets strong and pulsing; and a thermostat that maintains the water temperature whatever else is being used in the house.

Taps are available in an abundance of styles, and should be chosen carefully in their own right. They might be mounted on the wall or on the fixture itself, but make sure they are easy to handle, particularly with soapy hands, whether they are lever-operated, push-button or turned. Taps play an important part in finishing off the look of a bathroom, so it is worth spending time, money and effort finding the design that most appeals to you.

The next practical consideration is storage. Never underestimate your storage needs in the bathroom. Not only do you need somewhere for small items such as your toothbrush, toothpaste, shampoo, facial lotions, medicines and cotton swabs, but also you need a place to put those necessary but unsightly objects – toilet paper rolls, disinfectant, laundry and so on. Each object should be kept in a place convenient to where it is likely to be used. You might have storage cupboards or open shelves built into your scheme, or you might prefer to invest in free-standing pieces of furniture that will add to the visual interest as well as providing

LEFT AND ABOVE
Wood brings luxury to a room, particularly in bathrooms where it can evoke visions of ocean liners and grand yachts. Here, teak decking was chosen for the floor to give a contemporary look, as does the tongue-and-groove panelling. It was then teamed with the strong, hard lines of stone, stainless steel and chrome to play up the textural theme. A wall of opaque glass bricks creates a reflective shower cubicle, while slatted surfaces echo the decking.

storage space. Similarly, you might buy from a selection of bathroom furniture or think about customizing something you already own. Whatever your decision, consider what the furniture will bring to the scheme in a textural sense. Look at the surfaces and plan carefully what you are going to juxtapose it with to create the best effect.

Once you have chosen fixtures and furniture, it is time to think about décor. By keeping walls relatively plain – paint is a good choice – you can build up visual excitement through other surfaces, such as counters, panels, screens, doors, and floor. Because of the maintenance and durability factors, these will be mainly hard, but there is plenty of scope to mix in opaque with sheer, or matt with gloss.

Floors, for example, need to be water-resistant and easy to clean. Stone or ceramic tile floors are hard-wearing but cold underfoot, so you might consider investing in under-floor heating. Marble is too slippery for bathroom use, but slate and terrazzo are both slip-resistant. Exciting alternatives are available in carpet, but it is not worth considering in a bathroom for children. Teenagers also prefer a space where splashing and making a mess is tolerated, a far cry from the adult pleasures of enjoying a long, hot bath.

Windows should be dressed with privacy foremost in mind. This can be achieved easily with the use of sandblasted glass.

LEFT ABOVE AND BELOW
Bathrooms are often found to be cold rooms, full of hard, shiny surfaces. But it is easy to inject warmth with wood, cane and clay. Here, a bamboo ladder has been used as a towel holder, and a wooden bath rack and mat minimize the effect of cool wall tiles.

RIGHT
A cane-and-wood surround creates a comfortable feeling in this elegant bathroom, and is a perfect foil to the hardness of the marble counter. The ottoman has been covered in thick towelling fabric, which is functional and texturally effective.

Louvred shutters or pinoleum blinds are also ideal, but you might like to dress the windows more than this to introduce and accentuate softness in the room. Wispy sheers or symmetrical banners are alternative ways of doing this. If, however, the bathroom is well insulated, warm and not overlooked, you might prefer to do the opposite and have nothing at the windows at all.

Finally, you need to think about how to build up the textural elements in order to increase the feeling of luxury. A bathroom gives you scope for exciting combinations of glass, wood, steel, ceramics, mosaic tiles, decking, mirrors, glass bricks, marble and stone. You can experiment with textiles – perhaps by covering an ottoman in towelling fabric. Then continue the textural theme with the accessories you choose – wicker, metal, ceramic, fabric, wood or glass can all be used, and if they are placed next to contrasting textures will achieve maximum impact.

Once all this is done, you can add music, candles, your favourite bath oils, a glass of wine and flowers. In my perfect bathroom you would surround yourself with scents and tactile elements that make you feel calm, peaceful and spiritual. Every element should be chosen with care, because this is where you nurture yourself rather than others. You should feel uplifted every time you walk into your bathroom.

LEFT	RIGHT
The delicate pleats in this Fortuny-style fabric ripple like water. This sort of fabric has such a sensuous, organic feel that it is a essential to many of my schemes. For maximum impact, team it with something simple, such as felt or plain cotton.	*In a guest bathroom, you might prefer to keep the character of the room cool, clean and ultra-chic. Here, a limestone floor and unit have been lit softly to play up the natural beauty of the material. Only a slim line of mosaic tiles breaks up the solidity.*

STOCKISTS

The following suppliers are recommended for particular products in relation to this book. However, they all supply a variety of quality goods and fabrics.

Abbot & Boyd
8 Chelsea Harbour
Design Centre
London SW10 OXE
Tel: 0171 351 9985
linens, sheers and voiles, tafetta

Alex Begg & Co
Viewfield Road
Ayr
Scotland KA8 8HJ
Tel: 01292 267 615
Cashmere

Andrew Martin
200 Walton Street
London SW3 2JL
Tel: 0171 584 4290
Ethnic and textured fabrics, Kelly Hoppen Fabric Collection

Armourcoat
Harmer House
9 Harmer Street
Gravesend
Kent DA12 2AP
Tel: 01474 328 746
Special plaster finishes

Atrium
22–24 St Giles
High Street
London WC2H 8LN
Tel: 0171 375 7288
Contemporary furniture, lighting, suede

Attica
543 Battersea Park Road
London SW11 3BL
Tel: 0171 228 5785
Limestone, marble

B. Brown
74–78 Wood Lane End
Hemel Hempstead
Herts HP2 4RF
Tel: 08705 340 340
Felt

Bennett Silks
Crown Royal Park
Higher Hillgale
Stockport SK1 3HB
Tel: 0161 476 8600
Satin, silks

Bill Amberg
The Workshop
23 Theatre Street
Battersea
London SW11 5ND
Tel: 0171 924 4296
Leather, vellum

Bosanquet Ives
First floor
3 Court Lodge
48 Sloane Square
London SW1W 8AT
Tel:0171 730 6241
Floor coverings

Bruno Triplet Showroom
Unit 1, first floor
Chelsea Harbour
Design Centre
London SW10 OXE
Tel: 0171 795 0395
Linen, mohair, textured fabrics

Chelsea Glass
650 Portslade Road
London SW8 3DH
Tel: 0171 720 6905
Glass specialists

Chelsea Textiles
7 Walton Street
London SW3 2JD
Tel: 0171 584 0111.
Crewelwork, embroidery

Christian Liaigre
Showroom 1–61
Rue De Varenne
Showroom 2–42
Rue de Bac, 7th
Paris 75007, France
Tel: 01 4753 7876
Contemporary furniture and lighting

Claremont
29 Elystan Street
London SW3 3NT
Tel: 0171 581 9575
Hand-coloured and specialist fabrics, silk

Contemporary Aesthetics
301b Aberdeen House
22–24 Highbury Grove
London N5 2EA
Tel: 0171 226 5935
Contemporary furniture

Creation Baumann
41–42 Berners Street
London W1P 3AA
Tel: 0171 637 0253
Contemporary textured fabrics

Crucial Trading
79 Westbourne
Park Road
London W2
Tel: 0171 221 9000
Natural floor coverings

David Linley
Furniture Ltd
60 Pimlico Road
London SW1W 8LP
Tel: 0171 730 7300
Commissioned furniture

STOCKISTS

De Le Cuona Designs
1 Trinity Place
Windsor
Berkshire SL4 3AP
Tel: 01753 830 301
Linen

Domus Tiles
33 Parkgate Road
London SW11 4NP
Tel: 0171 223 5555
Glass, mosaics, tiles

Donghia
23 Chelsea Harbour
Design Centre
London SW10 OXE
Tel: 0171 823 3456
Contemporary furniture,
textured fabrics

Edgar Udny
314 Balham High Street
London SW17 7AA
Tel: 0181 767 8181
Mosaics

Erco Lighting
38 Dover Street
London W1X 3RD
Tel: 0171 408 0320
Lighting specialists

Farrow & Ball
Uddens Trading Estate
Wimborne
Dorset BH21 7NA
Tel: 01202 876 141
Paint

Fired Earth
Twyford Mill
Oxford Road
Adderbury
Oxfordshire OX17 3HP
Tel: 01295 814 300
Paint, including Kelly
Hoppen Paint Collection

F. R. Street
Frederick House
Hurricane Way
Wickford Business Park
Wickford
Essex SS11 8YB
Tel: 01268 766 677
Calico, linen, scrim

General Trading
Company
144 Sloane Street
London SW1X 9BL
Tel: 0171 730 0411
Horn products

Holland & Sherry
9–10 Saville Row
London W1X 1AF
Tel: 0171 437 0404
Wool

J Robert Scott
Unit 19 Second Floor
Chelsea Harbour
Design Centre
London SW10 OXE
Tel: 0171 376 4705
Contemporary furniture,
silks, textured fabrics

JAB International
1–15/16
Chelsea Harbour
Design Centre
London SW10 OXE
Tel: 0171 349 9323
Velvet

Jagtar
Unit 3–11
Chelsea Harbour
Design Centre
London SW10 OXE
Tel: 0171 351 4220
Silk, tafetta

John Cullen Lighting
585 Kings Road
London SW6 2EH
Tel: 0171 371 5400
Lighting specialists

H.V. Caldicott
Suite 2
Charan House
18 Union Street
London SW4 6JP
Tel: 020 7627 8787
Ribbon

Kravet
G17 Chelsea Harbour
Design Centre
London SW10 OXE
Tel: 0171 795 0110
Upholstery chenilles

Lelievre
1–19 Chelsea Harbour
Design Centre
London SW10 OXE
Tel: 0171 352 4798
Alacantara, suede

Libeco Lagae
Postbus 64
Tieltstraat 112
8760 Meulenbeke
Belgium
Tel: 05 148 8921
Linen

Limestone Gallery
2 Plimsoll Road
London N4 2EW
Tel: 0171 359 4432
Limestone specialists

Locharron
Waverley Mill
Galashiels
TD1 3AY
Tel: 01896 751 100
Cashmere

Malabar
31–33 The South Bank
Business Centre
Ponton Road
London SW8 5BL
Tel: 0171 501 4200
Cotton, tafetta

STOCKISTS

Manuel Canovas
2 North Terrace
Brompton Road
London SW3 2BA
Tel: 0171 225 2298
Cotton, velvet, wool

Mark Brazier-Jones
Hyde Hall Barn
Sandon, Buntingford
Hertfordshire SG9 0RU
Tel: 01763 273 599
*Modern furniture and
lighting*

Mary Fox Linton
1–10 Chelsea Harbour
Design Centre
London SW10 0XE
Tel: 0171 351 9908
Sheers, silk, suede

Nicholas Haslam
12 Holbein Place
London SW1 8NL
Tel: 0171 730 8623
*Chenille, contemporary
furniture, moleskin*

Olicana Textiles Ltd
Brook Mills
Crimble
Slaithwaite
Huddersfield HD7 5BQ
Tel: 01484 847 666
Cotton

Paul Glover Furniture
Unit 4 Backfield Farm
Wotton Road
Iron Acton
Near Bristol BS17 1XD
Tel: 0117 941 4600
Commissioned furniture

Pierre Frey
251–253 Fulham Road
London SW3 6HY
Tel: 0171 376 5599
Cotton

Ralph Lauren
Designers Guild
3 Olaf Street
London W11 4BE
Tel: 0171 229 1000
Cotton

Rentmeister
134 Lots Road
London SW10 0RJ
Tel: 0171 351 4333
Chenille

Roger Oates
The Long Barn
Eastnor, Ledbury
Hertfordshire HR8 1EL
Tel: 01531 631 611
Linen

Russell & Chapple
23 Monmouth Street
London WC2H 9DE
Tel: 0171 836 7521
Calico, linen, scrim

Sabina Fay Braxton
For orders:
11 Villa Leblanc
92120 Montrouge
Showroom:
5 Rue Daguerre
75014 Paris
France
Tel: 01 4657 1162
*Hand-coloured and
specialist fabrics*

Sahco Hesslein
Unit G24
Chelsea Harbour
Design Centre
Chelsea Harbour
London SW10 0XE
Tel: 0171 352 6168
*Mohair, sheers and voiles,
textured fabrics*

Snap Dragon
247 Fulham Road
London SW3 6HY
Tel: 0171 376 8889
*Chinese furniture and
accessories*

Spencer Fung
43 Pall Mall Deposit
128 Barlby Road
London W10 6BL
Tel: 0181 960 9883
Contemporary furniture

Taylors Prop
1 Silver Place
London W1R 3LL
Tel: 0171 437 1016
Buttons

The Nine Schools
Company
Ifield Gallery
121 Ifield Road
London SW10 9AR
Tel: 0171 835 2202
*Chinese furniture and
accessories*

V.V. Rouleaux
54 Sloane Square
London SW1W 8AX
Tel: 0171 730 3125
Ribbon

Wolfin Textiles
64 Great
Titchfield Street
London W1P 7AE
Tel: 0171 636 4949
Calico, linen, scrim

Zimmer Rhode
15 Chelsea
Garden Market
Chelsea Harbour
London SW10 0XE
Tel: 0171 351 7115
*Contemporary sheers
and voiles*

INDEX

Page numbers in *italic* refer to the illustrations

INDEX

ACKNOWLEDGMENTS

AUTHOR'S ACKNOWLEDGMENTS

With special thanks to all my clients who allowed me back into their homes to photograph, without them this book would not have been possible.

I would like to acknowledge Bill for creating the most beautiful photography, yet again: John Carter who reads my mind so accurately: Arabella McNie for her total professionalism: Helen Chislett who had the difficult task of interpreting my thoughts on paper: my husband Ed and my daughter Natasha for putting up with me and being so generous in their encouragement throughout the last year: and Alex for running everything to perfection.

THE AUTHOR WOULD ALSO LIKE TO THANK THE FOLLOWING WHO SUPPLIED MATERIAL FOR PHOTOGRAPHY:

Interiors Bis, Maxfield Parish, Nicole Farhi, Snap Dragon, The Conran Shop, The General Trading Company, Yeoward South

PUBLISHERS ACKNOWLEDGMENTS

The publisher would like to thank the following photographers and organisations for their kind permission to reproduce the photographs in this book:

10 Piero Biasion: **11** Alex Maclean/Photonica: **12** Robert O'Dea: **14 above** Carlos Navajas: **14 centre** Marianne Majerus (Design: Charles Jencks): **14 below** Kameo/Photonica: **16** Carlos Navajas /The Image Bank: **17 left** Stephen Miller: **17 right** Robert O'Dea: **20 above** Carlos Navajas: **20 below** Paul Ryan/International Interiors: **20–21 centre** Carlos Navajas: **22** Lucien Hervé (Arch: Le Corbusier): **24** Angelo Hornak: **24–25 centre** Paul Ryan/International Interiors: **25** Neo Vision/Photonica: **26** Richard Bryant/Arcaid (Courtesy of Schindler's Lifts): **27** Dick Scott-Stewart/The Special Photographers Library: **28–29 main picture** Yann Arthus Bertrand/Impact: **30 left** Piero Biasion: **30–31 main picture** Piero Biasion: **32–34** Piero Biasion: **80 right** Steven Edson/Photonica: **86** Piero Biasion: **93 left** Brian David Stevens /The Special Photographers Library: **97 above** Carlos Navajas: **102** Kazuo Sakauchi/Photonica: **108 left** Alan Keohane/Impact: **113 above** Jim Holmes/Axiom Photographic Agency: **113 below** Carlos Navajas: **114** Paul Raftery/Arcaid (Guggenheim Museum, Spain, Arch: Frank Gehry): **123** Robyn Beeche: **124 above and below** Javed a Jafferji/Impact: **137 left** Carlos Navajas/The Image Bank: **140** 1999 Comstock Inc: **152** Michael Pollard (Design: Beverley Clark)/Craft Council

Commissioning Editor: **Denny Hemming**
Project Editor: **Paula Hardy**
Acting Project Editor & Editorial Assistant: **Maxine McCaghy**
Art Editor & Director of Special Photography: **Karen Bowen**
Stylist: **Arabella McNie**
Assistant to Mr Batten: **Giles Westley**
Flower arrangements: **John Carter**
Picture Researcher: **Clare Limpus**
Production: **Suzanne Sharpless**

First published in 1999
by Conran Octopus Limited
a part of Octopus Publishing Group
2–4 Heron Quays
London E14 4JP
www.conran-octopus.co.uk
Reprinted 2000
Text © Kelly Hoppen 1999
Special photography © Bill Batten 1999
Design and layout © Conran Octopus Limited 1999

A catalogue record for this book is available from the British Library.
ISBN 1 84091 067 4
Printed in China